RATING HUNDREDS
OF THE BEST FILMS FOR
HOME VIDEO & CABLE

BEEKMAN HOUSE
New York

Manufactured in the United States of America
10 9 8 7 6 5 4 3 2 1

Library of Congress Catalog Card Number: 82-61433
ISBN: 0-517-398710

This edition published by:
Beekman House
Distributed by Crown Publishers, Inc.
One Park Avenue
New York, New York 10016

CONTENTS

Alphabetical Movie Listings

Star Profiles

CONTENTS

INTRODUCTION

What is an Adult Film?

What is an adult film? Who watches them? And why? These questions are foremost in the mind of anyone trying to understand this new phenomenon. Depicting the erotic impulse is nothing new. But the desire of the general public for entertainment that mirrors and expands upon their once forbidden dreams has mushroomed into a booming new industry. An adult film is a feature-length film that shows, with varying degrees of candor, human lovemaking. It may be a comedy, a drama, or even a documentary. Clearcut distinctions, however, are impossible. New markets have brought varying standards. Cable television shows adult films that are generally less graphic than the type available on videocassette. There can be no question, though, that the overwhelming success of these markets has proven the acceptance and popularity of sex-oriented films.

These changing attitudes have created a void. A multitude of films are released with little more than publicity to guide the audience about their quality. This book attempts to define new standards by which to judge the adult cinema.

There are, at present, very few adult films that can match the quality of commercial cinema. Only by recognizing and praising the good adult films (and damning the bad) can the public influence the quality of adult films it receives. The overall quality has risen dramatically in the last four years or so. The pressure of the new markets will force the quality to rise even further.

Considering the relatively low profile kept by the adult film industry, one is shocked to learn just how large the numbers are. Twenty-five to forty percent of all videocassettes sold are X-rated. The Adult Film Association of America estimates that adult films generate over $150 million dollars worth of business a year. With so much money at stake, it is surprising that few film reviews of new releases appear. That public scrutiny and critical judgment should escape an entire field of entertainment is unbelievable. The two best-selling films so far—*Deep Throat* and *Debbie Does Dallas*—are not, alas, the best. The enormous success of those films is more of a testament to the public's desires and to the types of films it would like to see than to the films themselves. All that is changing now. The public wants to be better informed.

As the early seventies were the period when adult films first became socially acceptable, films made during or before that period vary wildly in moral tone and degree of explicitness. Films made in the late seventies and eighties—the Golden Age—display little attempt to 'justify' sex, but merely portray it in the abundance and richness with which sex exists in real life. It is this attempt to accurately recreate our entire sexual milieu that hints at the answer to the second question, who watches these films? Adult films are now acceptable in all walks of life. All income levels, all education levels, all social levels are participating equally. While there are still more men than women who patronize adult films, women do constitute at least a third of the audience. And the number of women viewers is constantly on the rise. The myth of the sleazy pervert in a raincoat dies hard, but statistics show that the adult film audience is every bit as normal as a television audience. If anything, they may be more self-assured and determined, because they have had to overcome great difficulties to get the product they desire.

We can cite statistics to show that the public is watching these films, but saying why is much more subjective. Why did the collective mores of Americans shift towards watching sex acts in the seventies? We only know that they did. *Deep Throat* broke the dam, and the box-office, in 1972. The term "porno-chic" was coined in an attempt to explain why very respectable people were lining up at porno theatres. The trend of the day never died down, however. Only the attendant publicity dwindled. The social acceptability of sex might be explained in the events of the sixties, perhaps, but from where comes the desire to see it on the screen? The psychological reasons are bound up in cinema itself.

From the moment that Theda Bara looked into the camera with her big, dark eyes and pouting lips (back in 1913), audiences have been making love to the movie screen. Star worship, love stories, and the portrayal of sex have always been bound up culturally in the times. Our erotic imaginations derive, in part, from the sexuality we learn in movies. In previous generations, the movies have always led up to lovemaking, but never beyond. We learned courtship, kissing, and various other subliminal mating techniques by watching the stars. Up until the seventies, bedroom techniques were not considered a general knowledge that the movies could impart. But the desire to see the sex act on the screen is as fundamental as the desire to see a kiss. Human beings have the most complex mating rituals of any species; the desire to master these rituals continues beyond puberty as a constant aspect of the sex life. An adult film functions in much the same way a horror film does. Just as the audience of a horror film allows themselves to be scared in order to experience the emotions of that fear, the audience of an adult film permits themselves to be aroused in order to experience mentally the machinations of lovemaking. A person unwilling to be scared cannot enjoy a horror film; someone unwilling to become aroused will not find any value in an adult film.

The History of the Adult Film

The history of the adult film is the marriage of two separate strains — mainstream exploitation films and "stag" movies. The stag movies go back as far as film itself. The famous French postcards simply translated their poses onto film. The earliest known of these is *Le Bain*, 1896, in which an actress simply disrobes. By 1908, one-reelers with titles like *Making Love in a Hammock*, *A Seaside Flirtation*, or *Parisienne's Bedtime* were enacting humorous skits with sex for a finale. By 1915, the form of the stag film was set. A sophomoric situation and pun-ladden intertitles were the prelude to a sexual encounter, usually shot in a single camera take. These films quickly became the standard fare in brothels the world over, though production was regional with little distribution of films across national borders. When sixteen-millimeter film equipment became available, the stag party, or "smoker," was born.

Eight-millimeter films took stag films to the home market and even more localized distribution. From 1915 to 1970 there was little change in the stag film except that the miniscule plots grew smaller or disappeared. The "loop" film — non-stop sex action with no reference to plot that played continuously in a loop — was born. The fact that stag films remained silent meant that films made in the twenties remained in distribution into the sixties. Though everyone knows that Marilyn Monroe sidelined in stag films before heading for Hollywood, the only stag film to rise above the anonymous horde is *Smart Alec*, starring Candy Barr and made in 1951. The film is typical, but its publicity was not, and *Smart Alec* became the most widely distributed stag film. There have been persistent rumors that stag versions of passionate Hollywood films like *Red Dust* were made, with stand-ins for Jean Harlow and Clark Gable performing the lustful deeds. None of these versions have ever been found, however.

The mainstream exploitation pictures began in the early thirties with sexy pre-Hayes Code teen pictures like *Hot Saturday*. The term, "exploitation picture," is not derogatory, but simply refers to a marketing technique. Some of the best-loved films fall into this category. They resurfaced in the late thirties under the guise of educational films which have since become camp classics with leering titles like *Reefer Madness*. The forties were filled with B-movies, which seemed to have fulfilled the desire for low-class entertainment. Exploitation bounced back in the fifties bigger than ever with biker movies, beach movies, sci-fi movies, monster movies, and rock-n-roll movies, each more leering and titillating than the next. Into this scene came Russ Meyer, who in 1959 made *The Immoral Mr. Teas*. Mr. Teas was a Walter Mitty type who spied upon and ogled naked women. This was the first publicly-exhibited film that showed nudity. The nudity was allowed because no sex was involved. Russ Meyer was the first to introduce exploitation films for the adult, rather than teen, market. From this inauspicious beginning the barriers began to fall with each new picture. Russ Meyer's 1964 *Lorna* was the first film to show nudity and sex; and his 1968 *Vixens* was the first adult film hit. Meyer's brand of entertainment was big on huge breasts, fast talk, fast action, and fast editing. The violence of the style was often matched by the violence in the story, but there can be no doubt that Russ Meyer charted a personal course that was extremely influential on other adult filmmakers.

Another filmmaker that broke through the moral barriers in the chaotic sixties was Radley Metzger. Metzger entered the market by distributing the Danish film, *I, A Woman*, and went on to make his own films. Metzger is the link between the sixties softcore titillation and the modern adult film. Indeed, Radley Metzger is the director (under the pseudonym Henri Paris) of the 1976 masterpiece, *The Opening of Misty Beethoven*—universally acclaimed as the finest adult film yet made.

The late sixties saw Hollywood making X-rated films and the creation of "porno theaters" that exhibited exclusively X- and XXX-rated films. An X-rating was earned for frontal nudity or simulated sex. XXX depicted an erection or penetration. It was in these days that the myth of the seedy raincoated pervert-patron was born.

That myth was exploded in June 1972, when an unprepossessing film called *Deep Throat*, shot in six days for $24,000, opened at Bob Sumner's New World Theatre in Times Square, New York critics gave the film prominent favorable notice, and the film took off—as box-office hit and media event. Linda Lovelace became a celebrity overnight. *Deep Throat* played for 365 consecutive weeks in L.A., and is reported to have earned nearly $100 million dollars so far. Its influence spilled over even into the Watergate affair (Woodward and Bernstein's supersecret contact was code-named "Deep Throat"). The attendent hoopla gave an excuse to those leery of gossip to see an adult film. Apparently, the public liked what it saw. Other XXX-rated hits followed: *Behind the Green Door*, *The Devil in Miss Jones*, and *The Resurrection of Eve*. These films paved the way for explicit art films like *Last Tango in Paris*, which starred Marlon Brando in an obsessive relationship with Maria Schneider.

The blossoming atmosphere, dubbed "porno-chic," soured somewhat in 1973 when the Supreme Court decided that local communities could set their own standards of obscenity. The impending possibility of big budget Hollywood adult films that *Deep Throat* had portended stalled. No one wanted to risk being jailed in Peoria. But the impending backlash from conservative circles that everyone expected never materialized. Harry Reems was indicted in Memphis by a headline hungry D.A., but was acquitted easily.

By far the most significant event in adult-film history was in 1976 when Sony unveiled the videocassette machine. The home videocassette machine meant that "local standards" were reduced to an audience of one. Anyone was free to choose what type of material he/she would like to see. Immediately, adult films were made available on cassette and sold well at a whopping $300 per tape. Price wars and a glut of products have brought the price per cassette down to approximately the cost of normal films, but demand for adult films has never decreased since their introduction. The spreading of cable systems widened the availability even further (there are currently 4500 separate cable systems in operation). Adult filmmakers found that they were even more popular than when they had been chic.

The years 1976-1979 separated the serious producers, ready to cater to their new middle class market, from the amateurs. Film budgets rose from the under $25,000—that *Deep Throat* and its like were made for—to over $125,000. Cinematography, acting, writing, and sets improved dramatically. Films with superior values like *Babyface, Babylon Pink, Candy Stripers, Misty Beethoven* and *Take-Off* began to surface. Veterans Radley Metzger and Alex DeRenzy competed with newcomers Svetlana, Armand Weston, and Henri Pachard for the talents of stars like Annette Haven, Marilyn Chambers, Harry Reems, John Holmes, Seka, and Jamie Gillis.

The last three years have seen even further improvement in style. Filmmakers are beginning to experiment with complicated narrative forms; the male-oriented nature of the sex is being subjugated in order to attract more women. Breakthrough films of the last few years include: *Talk Dirty to Me, Ecstasy Girls, Nightdreams, Neon Nights,* and *Nothing to Hide.* The bright new stars of the scene are directors Anthony Spinelli and Rinse Dream (pseudonyms still persist), and stars John Leslie, Veronica Hart, Susan Nero, and Drea.

Defining an Aesthetic

Defining an aesthetic of the adult film is difficult because the early work is concerned with pushing contemporary mores to the limits and the current work is in a state of flux adjusting to its new audiences and increased budgets. Needless to say, however, this is the most exciting time to be studying the genre. An interested and informed public still has an enormous input toward defining the style that will emerge.

From the outset, we should emphasize that an adult film is not pornography. Pornography is a work that is obscene, that transcends the moral codes of its society. Our society has changed such in recent years that works once considered obscene are no longer. (There still exist moral standards in our culture, and there still exists pornography that flaunts it.)

Five major factors influence the outcome of a successful adult film: the plot, the actors, the sex, the presence or absence of humor, and the production values. There is yet no formula for a perfect adult film, no recipe for the ingredients. One can say conclusively, however, that the recent improvement in total product has resulted in a uniform improvement in the five major factors.

The plots have developed from practically non-existant in the vignette films (where a threadbare narrative ties together completely unrelated sexual encounters) to the rich complexity of *Ecstasy Girls*, where the sexual escapades are integral to the development of the story. Falling somewhere in between, most films deal with a particular sex fantasy theme: nurses, cheerleaders, teenyboppers, cowgirls, or lesbians. Also very popular are take-off spoofs of mainstream films and detective stories. The dialogue has also progressed from lame-brained ad-libbing to a coherent simplicity. The next big step is into genuinely witty dialogue, which a few films have begun to attempt.

The acting in the early adult films was such that we immediately understood why stag films remained silent for all those years. *Deep Throat* was aided by the fact that Linda Lovelace's mouth was occupied most of the time and the affable Harry Reems got the best lines. The increased limelight of the seventies forced the lesser talents and undesirables to fade away. Today's stars are more colorful and their own personalities are allowed to rise through in their films.

The sex burst out, as hardcore as can be, in *Deep Throat*. After that, there was nowhere to go, except to get kinkier or more subtle. Through the seventies, the sex remained constant. Bondage, rape, and anal intercourse were prevalent, but the filmmakers themselves seemed to be defining the limits of taste, based on their experience. No bondage or rape was ever physically harmful, and no illegal perversions ever entered into the mainstream adult films. The new trend now is towards subtler treatment of the sex acts. The semi-ridiculous orgasm shots are dying out. The cinematography is less gynecological and more erotic. The varieties of interpersonal experience remain as wide as individual preference. And there has been a greater effort to work the circumstances of the sexual encounter into the story. Correctly assuming that induced lovemaking is more stimulating and erotic than random sex, the filmmakers are proceeding apace.

Humor in adult films goes all the way back to the sophomoric intertitles of stag films. There was a shade of subtlety in Russ Meyer's hypocritical moralizing at the end of his films. The pompous overtones served the dual function of excusing the sex and nudity to the censors and providing laughs for his audience (who knew he wasn't the least bit sincere). The camp-to-death gagging of *Deep Throat* set the tone for the numerous comedies that followed. But there were only so many lame jokes to go around and, inevitably, the humor improved.

Production values are something that only a film buff might pin down, but that everyone notices subliminally. The luxury of flesh-toned flesh and sets that include more than a bed do not make a film in themselves, but rather allow us to maintain the filmic illusion in our mind. It is very hard to be swept into a fantasy world when the microphone boom is clearly evident in the shot. To say that production budgets are rising is the clearest indication that production values are going up, too.

The Future

Where adult cinema will go from here is still an open question. Whether the films continue to improve to the point where we might talk about an 'alternative Hollywood,' or whether Hollywood finally jumps in and co-opts the industry will be determined in the next five years. The cable, cassette, and videodisc industries will only expand further. They might enter production themselves, capitalizing on the pioneering breakthroughs of the independents. Already, production companies have begun to produce adult movies directly on videotape, bypassing theaters and going straight to the cassette and television markets. This new technology will result in warmer, more pleasing fleshtones and a generally improved television image. The plots will grow more subtle still in an attempt to lure more women. More film time will be given over to seduction, perhaps dipping for plots into the Gothic romances (whose steamy sex scenes are made to order for adult cinema). Hollywood's lost love, the romantic comedy, may also find a home in the adult cinema. What effect will all this have on our culture? Some experts are predicting a second sexual revolution, with adult cinema knocking down the last doors of hyprocrisy and repression. Soothsayer Issac Asimov is predicting that widespread acceptance of an adult cinema will lead to a time when an individual's sex life, in intimate detail, will become an ordinary topic of social conversation.

Such improved social benefits depend upon an informed public molding its adult cinema into a truly representative and artistic mirroring of its own creative sexual urges. The stag film dies hard, but the new age looms ahead.

RATING THE ADULT FILMS

There have been over 8000 adult films made over the years. Approximately 2000 are available on videocassette. The 200 plus films selected for inclusion represent the top 2.5% of all adult films made. You can rest assured that simply by inclusion in this volume we are claiming that a film is better than the other 97.5% of mostly drivel. Two-hundred is an arbitrary figure, however, and it is unavoidable that some personal favorites will be omitted. Beyond mere inclusion, each film is rated on a four-star system, with one star being watchable, two stars recommended, three stars a must-see, and four-stars a masterpiece. In addition, each film is rated individually on a ten-point, quick comparison chart that judges: Directing, Casting, Acting, Script, Theme, Humor, Production Values, and lists Year of Production, Running Time, and Genre. This will enable the viewer to quickly determine a film's value based upon his/her own preference. For example, one might easily discover all the Cheerleader films by checking the Theme section of the charts.

The films have been divided into three basic categories: Graphic, Erotic, and Taboo. Graphic includes mostly XXX films and films that fully display the sex act. If in the review, a Graphic film is referred to as Explicit, then one must be prepared for close-ups of the act and other extreme portrayals. In most instances, particularly shocking scenes will be noted. The Erotic category includes Softcore, X-, and R-rated films. These films are characterized by a more romanticized treatment of sex. The Taboo category includes films that are not necessarily erotic, but are definitely adult. These films are often cult or comic in nature. However, they do contain shocking acts, camp behavior, nudity, nonerotic sex, and perhaps violence. Andy Warhol and John Waters are two practitioners of the taboo genre. They are labeled Taboo because their primary intent is to probe the social and moral limits.

The reviews are concise and informative, containing in most cases an evaluation of the film, a description of the plot, and a rundown on the type of sexual activity depicted. The book also contains Star Profiles, biographies of your favorite adult film actors and actresses listing their character traits and backgrounds, and their biggest films. Enjoy Rating the Adult Films.

EDITORS AND AUTHORS

Kent Smith moved to Los Angeles in 1978 pursuing a writing/photography career. Soon after his arrival, he got a job as assistant and contributing editor on "Adam Film World," a magazine that covers the adult film industry, and he began covering many of the adult films' premiers and interviewing various personalities connected in the business.

After a brief period as an editor at Knight Publications, where he put out many pictorial and specialty magazines, he began to work full time as a freelance writer/photographer.

Darrell W. Moore is both a writer on film and a filmmaker. He has worked as a research assistant for the Film Center of the Art Institute of Chicago. He has published several critical studies of films and writes reviews for several magazines. Mr. Moore holds a B.F.A. in filmmaking, and has produced six short films thus far. His films, *Quantum* and *Starting in the Middle of the Day, We Can Drink Our Politics* are in distribution by the Filmmaker's Co-Op in New York.

Merl Reagle, comes to editing through the legendary back door. Although he is nationally known as a member of the Crossword Elite (he makes puzzles for *Games* Magazine, Dell, Simon and Schuster, et al.), his long news editing experience and educated taste in movies made him an ideal choice for this guide. Reagle is also a Hollywood screenwriter, songwriter, and synthesizer freak who is known in his Santa Monica neighborhood as the "Old Missile Commander."

★ Watchable	★★★ Must See
★★ Recommended	★★★★ Masterpiece

AFTERNOON DELIGHTS ★

Director: Warren Evans
Cast: Eric Edwards, Merle Michaels, Veronica Hart,
  Vanessa Del Rio

Despite some well-crafted erotic encounters, this is a standard adult film.

Afternoon Delights is about five young men who play poker every Tuesday evening. The group's self-imposed leader decides to do something different: He gives the players sheets of paper and tells each one to write down an incident where his wife has been unfaithful. He then gathers the sheets and places them in a hat. Each player in turn picks out one of the pieces of paper and reads it out loud, and they all bet on who the husband is. Of course, while each event is being read we cut to it in live action.

One woman teases a whole construction crew. Another has an affair with her dentist and his female assistant, making a very exciting threesome. Another woman has nocturnal fantasies involving copulation with strangers in a theater. Another woman is a timid librarian who gets her kicks by becoming a leather-clad dominatrix during lunch. The last housewife auditions for an adult film and gets the lead.

The major failing of the film is its loose story which, after a couple of incidents, loses its forward drive. Eric Edwards is very effective as the kinky idea man, and Veronica Hart and Vanessa Del Rio are quite convincing as sex-crazed, bored housewives.

Genre: Graphic
Year: 1981
Time: 80 min.
Acting: Fair
Casting: Good

Script: Fair
Production: Good
Directing: Good
Theme: Housewives
Humor: Yes

A

ALICE IN WONDERLAND ★★★

Director: Bud Townsend
Cast: Kristine DeBell, Terri Hall, Juliet Graham, Nancy Dare

This erotic, musical version of the Lewis Carroll classic is well crafted and brightly creative.

A lovely librarian, played by Playboy model Kristine De-Bell, falls asleep and dreams herself into a strange world filled with extremely uninhibited people. These people love to sing and dance and fool around. Alice has a series of sensual adventures among these characters.

The film was originally shot as an ode to eroticism with few explicit sex scenes, which were eventually cut from its theatrical release. Videocassette versions, however, have had some of the original erotic encounters spliced back in them.

For an extremely low-budget picture, the makers of this film did an excellent job. The cinematography is vibrant, the dances and numbers quite professional, and the acting adorable. Without a doubt, it is one of the best adult fairytales and/or musicals around.

Genre: Erotic
Year: 1976
Time: 88 min.
Acting: Good
Casting: Very Good

Script: Very Good
Production: Good
Directing: Very Good
Theme: Librarian
Humor: Yes

ALL ABOUT GLORIA LEONARD ★★

Director: Gloria Leonard
Cast: Gloria Leonard, Jamie Gillis, Gloria Todd

This pseudo-documentary on *High Society* magazine publisher Gloria Leonard is one of the better "inside" adult films.

In this film, Gloria looks into her past life, describing some of the more luscious points in vibrant, sexual explicitness. (Whether or not these incidents are true never seems to matter.) As an actress, Gloria is not bad, and quite accurately portrays herself as a gutsy, independent career woman. The sex scenes depict her as a woman of seemingly insatiable lust.

As a pseudo-doc, it works well. But as an adult movie, its production values and scenes are barely better than average, except for a famous interracial lesbian sequence. which is both erotic and comedic. Ultimately, the film hinges on Gloria Leonard's personality—either you like her or you don't.

Genre: Graphic
Year: 1978
Time: 108 min.
Acting: Fair
Casting: Good

Script: Fair
Production: Good
Directing: Fair
Theme: Gloria Leonard
Humor: No

★ Watchable   ★★★ Must See
★★ Recommended   ★★★★ Masterpiece

A

AMANDA BY NIGHT   ★★★

Director: Robert McCallum
Cast: Veronica Hart, Richard Bolla, Jamie Gillis,
  Lisa DeLeeuw, Samantha Fox

Despite this film's strong popularity, it is one of the few adult films in which the sex scenes are considered gratuitous even by fans of adult cinema. The story line is much stronger than the eroticism, and the film thus has a jagged or incomplete feeling.

The film is about a mad killer of high-class hookers. A no-nonsense cop, confidently portrayed by Richard Bolla, enlists the help of Amanda, a very elegant woman of the night, in his attempt to catch the killer. Amanda refuses to help the cop— until she discovers the killer is after her.

The film was produced and directed as adult entertainment, and contains a number of graphic sexual encounters between hookers and their clients, and between vice squad policemen and their female suspects. All the time spent on these sexual exploits detracts from the story. The elegant acting of Veronica Hart and the fine performance of Richard Bolla have made this film one of the most popular.

Genre: Graphic
Year: 1981
Time: 95 min.
Acting: Very Good
Casting: Good

Script: Good
Production: Good
Directing: Very Good
Theme: Prostitute
Humor: No

AMERICAN DESIRE ★★

Director: Lasse Brown
Cast: Veronica Hart, Richard Bolla, Mai Lin, Lisa Adams,
George Payne

This is a very sexy, high-quality, low-budget adult film. It doesn't cover anything new, but it's solid adult entertainment.

The story centers on the declining sexual interests of a couple living together (Veronica Hart and Richard Bolla). To find sexual fulfillment, both begin searching elsewhere, and we're carried through a number of very erotic interludes.

The sex is graphic and energetic with a special appearance of Oriental heartthrob Mai Lin, who really can't act, but emotes a lot of sensuality.

The film has a naturalness and believability rare in adult films. This is certainly due to the screen presence of its lead—Veronica Hart—who is quickly developing into a fine, sensual performer.

Genre: Graphic	**Script:** Fair
Year: 1981	**Production:** Good
Time: 78 min.	**Directing:** Good
Acting: Good	**Theme:** Swinging Couples
Casting: Good	**Humor:** No

★ Watchable ★★★ Must See
★★ Recommended ★★★★ Masterpiece

A

Director: Jeffrey Fairbanks
Cast: Arcadia Lake, Lysa Thatcher, Eric Edwards, Randy West

A superior story line and good performances made this a popular entry in 1981, but its slow pace makes it average overall.

The film is about two young losers who kidnap two girls to collect a big ransom from their rich father. The father, however, thinks they've staged the whole thing and refuses to pay. The punks become furious and make the girls themselves pay —sexually.

The plot offers a lot of room for erotic encounters between the captors and the captives, and these interludes contain a lot of graphic and indulgent sex, with a few quasi-bondage scenes thrown in.

The photography is quite nice, especially in the beginning as the two girls are on the way to their high school prom. Arcadia Lake and Lysa Thatcher are both very young looking, and quite believable as high school seniors spoiled rotten by the good life.

Genre: Graphic	**Script:** Good
Year: 1981	**Production:** Good
Time: 88 min.	**Directing:** Good
Acting: Fair	**Theme:** Adolescent Girls
Casting: Good	**Humor:** Yes

★ Watchable   ★★★ Must See
★★ Recommended   ★★★★ Masterpiece

JULIET ANDERSON

Like Georgina Spelvin, Juliet Anderson was much older than most women when she began her erotic acting career. Juliet Anderson had already spent quite a few years in Europe teaching English as a second language. It was during her stay in Europe that she was introduced to the wild and crazy lifestyle of sexual freedom.

On her return to the United States, she decided to experiment in something completely different. She had always been intrigued with adult films, and started looking into it. One of her first parts was the Swedish maid in Pretty Peaches, where her talents for both light comedy and heavy sex became apparent.

She starred in the Swedish Erotica Aunt Peg series, which was later made into a number of feature-length films. She has gone on to do a number of other films, including Randy, The Electric Lady, 8 to 4, Manhattan Mistress and Shoppe of Temptations. She has recently moved behind the camera, and her first directorial job was with an exclusive videocassette featured called All The Kings Ladies, soon to be released.

A

ANNA OBSESSED

Directors: Martin & Martin
Cast: Constance Money, John Leslie, Annette Haven,
  Susan McBain

Originally titled *Obsessed*, this film was not well received and
quickly withdrawn. It was then re-issued, slightly re-edited,
under the current title, but still it didn't do very well. Considering its slightly out-of-the ordinary story line, however, it
deserves an above average rating.

The story opens quite uninterestingly with a frustrated
housewife trying to find fulfillment. But the plot soon veers
into the exploits of a crazed rapist and the erotic nightmares of
another woman. Constance Money and Susan McBain resem-
ble each other, and sometimes the photography makes it difficult to figure out who is whom.

The sexual encounters are surprisingly sparse, but very
graphic and powerful when they do appear. Many of the
dream sequences are very original and sexually charged.

Genre: Graphic
Year: 1978
Time: 82 min.
Acting: Very Good
Casting: Good

Script: Good
Production: Good
Directing: Very Good
Theme: Rape
Humor: No

★ Watchable   ★★★ Must See
★★ Recommended   ★★★★ Masterpiece

THE ARABIAN NIGHTS ★★★

Director: Pier Paolo Pasolini
Cast: Ninetoo Davoli, Franco Merli, Ines Pelligrini,
Luigina Rocchi

This film version retains much of the eroticism in Sir Richard Burton's original translation, which previous film treatments saw fit to water down. Great care was taken in the details: it was shot on location (Africa and the Middle East) and a dark-skinned girl was cast as the princess. The acting is excellent, and the stories weave in and out in intriguing fashion.

The film selects some of the more popular of the Arabian Nights stories, but intertwines them in strange ways. Like the original, many stories lead into other stories and again into others.

One of the most erotic sequences is when two supernatural beings decide to play a trick on a virginal girl and boy. The beings make each young person seduce the other while he or she is asleep.

In another scene, one of the heroes finds himself in a pool with a bevy of very pretty, very nude Arabian women, who tease and tickle him into sensual rapture.

The sexual encounters in the film are boldly uninhibited, but not graphic or explicit. The film received its X rating more for its gory sequences, including a bloody castration, than for its sex, although that, too, added to the restriction.

Nevertheless, this film received a broad release throughout the United States and is a good example of the blending of mainstream and adult entertainment.

Genre: Erotic **Script:** Very Good
Year: 1974 **Production:** Fair
Time: 130 min. **Directing:** Excellent
Acting: Good **Theme:** Harem
Casting: Very Good **Humor:** Yes

A

AUTOBIOGRAPHY OF A FLEA

Director: Sharon McKnight
Cast: Jean Jennings, John Holmes, Paul Thomas,
   Annette Haven

Based on a novel written anonymously during the Victorian era, this movie concerns a young virgin's initiation into the delights of sex in 1810 France. Her first encounter is with a priest, and as repentance for her "sin" she must relieve the lusty desires of other members of the local clergy.

The erotic scenes are frequent and very intense, often at the expense of the story line. The film's strongest point is its mood—its care in handling the period—both in depicting the time's repressive attitude toward sex and the hypocrisy of the church fathers.

Genre: Graphic
Year: 1976
Time: 86 min.
Acting: Good
Casting: Good

Script: Good
Production: Very Good
Directing: Good
Theme: Priests and Virgins
Humor: No

BABY FACE ★★★

Director: Alex DeRenzy
Cast: Lyn Cuddles Malone, Amber Hunt, Linda Wong, Kristine Heller, Desiree Cousteau

Alex DeRenzy is one of the foremost members of the erotic underground, and this picture (along with *Pretty Peaches*) best illustrates his work. It is bizarre, humorous, and very erotic—a superior example of adult filmmaking.

A big, hard-working guy has a brief affair with a teenage girl, but her mother considers it rape and calls the cops. The big guy gets away and becomes a hustler in a cathouse that caters to rich women. Eventually, one of the women who comes into the cathouse is the girl's mother.

DeRenzy's vision of sex is often bizarre, always highly charged, thoroughly indulgent, and quite explicit. The film's highlight is with Kristine Heller, who plays a rock singer with a strong penchant for more than one man at a time.

A lot has been said about Alex DeRenzy, and his depictions of the erotically bizarre have left a definite mark on the adult film business.

Genre: Graphic
Year: 1977
Time: 85 min.
Acting: Very Good
Casting: Good

Script: Good
Production: Good
Directing: Very Good
Theme: Brothel
Humor: Yes

★ Watchable   ★★★ Must See
★★ Recommended   ★★★★ Masterpiece

B

BABYLON PINK

Director: Henri Pachard
Cast: Samantha Fox, Vanessa Del Rio, Georgina Spelvin

One of the standard formats for adult films is a loose story line that affords separate, unrelated sex vignettes. This is one of the best examples of the format.

The "story" concerns the erotic fantasies of a number of young women—housewife, teenager, business executive, secretary, socialite. This is a superactive, super-creative bunch, and the fantasies are extremely stimulating.

The picture won the Adult Film Association of America's best film award in 1979, which it richly deserved. It also marked the debut of Henri Pachard into erotic filmmaking.

Genre: Graphic
Year: 1979
Time: 87 min.
Acting: Fair
Casting: Good

Script: Fair
Production: Good
Directing: Very Good
Theme: Women's Fantasies
Humor: No

BAD (ANDY WARHOL'S)   ★★★

Executive Producer: Andy Warhol
Director: Jed Johnson
Cast: Carroll Baker, Perry King, Susan Tyrrell

Though Warhol films (not always directed by him) are always innovative, self-indulgent, and usually campy, this film comes closest to being a mainstream movie. It cost $1.5 million and stands out in remarkable contrast to Warhol's other films.

Mrs. Aiken (Carroll Baker) runs both a slummy facial-hair removal business and a murder-for-hire service that specializes in killing kids and animals. She doesn't do the murders herself; she has a team of assassins for that. She does, however, remove hair.

Needless to say, her dual endeavors make for some very strange sequences. One mother, for example, impatient that her hired killers haven't arrived, tosses her infant out the window herself.

The intention of all Warhol movies is to disturb or shock. They use sex, murder, comedy, decadence, perversion, and a variety of other techniques to do this. *Bad* is perhaps one of the better examples of his work.

Genre: Taboo
Year: 1971
Time: 100 min.
Acting: Good
Casting: Very Good

Script: Good
Production: Good
Directing: Very Good
Theme: Assassins
Humor: Yes

★   Watchable   ★★★   Must See
★★   Recommended   ★★★★   Masterpiece

B

BAD GIRLS ★★

Director: David Frazer and Svetlana
Cast: Pia Snow, Jasmine DuBay, Victoria Knoll, Lenora Bruce

Despite a terrific beginning, colorful photography, and some very pretty girls, *Bad Girls* is really just half a film, even for an adult movie.

Four young female models, one a photographer, head off to the forests of Northern California for a photo shooting. While navigating the mountain roads, they meet a Boy Scout whom they pick up and sexually tease. When they finally let him go, he tells his older brother about what happened, and the two boys return for revenge.

The sex scenes for the first part are excellently crafted. They tease rather than show, but quickly build into the traditional adult format.

The film has been extremely popular due to its fresh, pretty faces, delightful scenes and acting, and colorful wilderness photography, but its conventional second half is the cause of its average overall rating.

Genre: Graphic
Year: 1981
Time: 82 min.
Acting: Fair
Casting: Good

Script: Fair
Production: Good
Directing: Fair
Theme: Models, Boy Scouts
Humor: Yes

★ Watchable ★★★ Must See
★★ Recommended ★★★★ Masterpiece

BAD TIMING ★★★

Director: Nicolas Roeg
Cast: Theresa Russell, Art Garfunkel, Harvey Keitel

Cinematographer-turned-director Nicolas Roeg delves into erotic obsession in this film, with startling results. It rates high in production value and acting and has an innovative approach to an old story.

The film is basically a character study. Alex (Art Garfunkel) is a somber American psychoanalyst living in Vienna. Theresa Russell plays Milena, a vibrant, carefree American girl. They meet by chance at a party and are thrown into a roller-coaster ride of an erotic relationship. He wants to smash her free spirit because he can't understand it, but she won't let him. The result is a near-fatal break-up.

Roeg approaches the story from the middle (obeying Jean-Luc Godard's dictum, "A film must have a beginning, a middle and an end, but not necessarily in that order.") We rapidly move to the various parts of Alex and Milena's relationship, slipping through time as if it were Jell-O. The editing is intricate, but not confusing. As we move back and forth, we begin to see more clearly how these two unlikely lovers ever got together.

The film is filled with exceptional images. When the relationship is breaking up, the lovers take a trip to North Africa, the barren landscape outside accenting their situation.

The film was not well received on its release, which is a shame. Theresa Russell is exceptional.

Genre: Erotic
Year: 1980
Time: 123 min.
Acting: Excellent
Casting: Very Good

Script: Very Good
Production: Very Good
Directing: Excellent
Theme: Erotic Obsession
Humor: No

B

BALL GAME

Director: Ann Perry
Cast: Candida Royalle, Lisa DeLeeuw, Jennifer West,
Susan Nero

Despite its illogical premise and less than professional acting, this film still comes off as a fairly entertaining adult sex comedy.

A group of hookers are in the county jail. As should be expected in an adult film, the hookers are sexually used and abused by prison guards of both sexes. One of the girls complains to the warden, and is then sexually abused by the warden's fiery redheaded secretary. The warden decides to ease the tension by sponsoring a baseball game between the angry hookers and the guards. The game, of course, soon degenerates into a zany orgy.

The treatment of sex is quite traditional for an adult film. There are female guards romping with the inmates, quasi-rapes that turn into hot erotic action, threesomes, and loads of heterosexual game playing.

The girls are enthusiastic and easily excitable, but their acting is poor. Susan Nero, however, is quite effective as a dominant and sensually brutal guard, especially when she makes love to one of the hookers in the bathroom. And Lisa DeLeeuw is explosive as the foul-mouthed, sex-crazed secretary.

Genre: Graphic
Year: 1980
Time: 84 min.
Acting: Fair
Casting: Fair

Script: Poor
Production: Good
Directing: Fair
Theme: Hookers
Humor: Yes

BARBARA BROADCAST ★★★

Director: Henry Paris (Radley Metzger)
Cast: Annette Haven, C.J. Laing, Susan McBain, Wade Nichols

This film was voted by *Hustler* and *Screw* magazines as the best picture of 1977, and it was.

A posh restaurant offers not only food as part of its menu, but the waitresses and waiters as well. The plot, which is slight for a Paris film, uses an interview between a female reporter and a top-flight hooker as a jumping-off place for their encounters with the restaurant's exclusive clientele.

The film's raunchiest scene takes place in the kitchen, where C.J. Laing engages in "water sports" and "Greek" coupling. Most of the eroticism in the film, however, is of the Tom Jones variety, mixing food and sex in many different ways. It often gets quite messy.

The cinematography is surprisingly sophisticated for an adult film. Director Henry Paris is a veteran of erotic films in both Europe and America, and this is one of his jewels.

Genre: Graphic	**Script:** Good
Year: 1977	**Production:** Very Good
Time: 87 min.	**Directing:** Very Good
Acting: Good	**Theme:** Reporter
Casting: Good	**Humor:** Yes

★	Watchable	★★★	Must See
★★	Recommended	★★★★	Masterpiece

B

BEHIND THE GREEN DOOR

Producers/directors: Jim and Artie Mitchell
Cast: Marilyn Chambers, Johnnie Keyes, George S. McDonald

One of the top three underground classics, this film still attracts big audiences and sells an extraordinary amount of videocassettes. Its production values, photography, and acting are actually below average. For historical significance—the first appearance of the stunning Marilyn Chambers—and the film's continuing popularity, we give it two stars.

A trucker tells his buddy about a strange sex club he once attended where a young girl (Marilyn Chambers) was forced to participate in a sex show. The bulk of the film is a flashback to the show itself. After some initial anxiety, the girl willingly goes along with it.

Like many adult films, it spends too much time on the sex acts, and not enough on any kind of story. It was the first film that tried to be artistic and erotic, and a special effects shot near the end is interesting. Though its production values are below average by today's standards, it still is historically significant for Marilyn's vibrant adult debut.

Genre: Graphic
Year: 1972
Time: 72 min.
Acting: Fair
Casting: Good

Script: Fair
Production: Fair
Directing: Good
Theme: Abduction
Humor: No

BEL AMI ★★

Director: Bert Torn
Cast: Harry Reems, Christa Linder, Maria Lynn

This light comedy is based loosely on the novel by Guy de Maupassant.

Harry Reems plays an ambitious journalist working for a very strict and moral magazine. He is offered quite a sum of money to write poetry for a nudie magazine. At first he refuses, but later reconsiders and writes the poems. Soon he is hired by the nudie magazine as an editor. He eventually works his way to the top, seducing a couple of secretaries, a figure model, and the publisher's wife along the way.

The erotic encounters are presented in a teasing, titillating manner with surprisingly few graphic inserts, which seem to have been added for its American release. Reems is not a dynamic actor nor is he really a good one, but he is competent and has a flair for light comedy. He invokes sympathy from the audience quite easily. The supporting actresses don't do much acting, but they are very appealing and attractive, giving thoroughly sensual performances.

The movie is very upbeat and does not portray the journalist in the serious, downbeat manner of the book.

Genre: Graphic
Year: 1974
Time: 90 min.
Acting: Fair
Casting: Good

Script: Good
Production: Very Good
Directing: Fair
Theme: Secretaries, Reporters, Models
Humor: Yes

★ Watchable   ★★★ Must See
★★ Recommended   ★★★★ Masterpiece

B

BENEATH THE VALLEY OF THE ULTRAVIXENS ★★★

Director: Russ Meyer
Cast: Francesca "Kitten" Natividad, Anne Marie, Ken Kerr

This most recent entry in the Vixen series explores the Peyton Place-like world of sex and sin.

An on-screen narrator gives us the rundown on the inhabitants of a small southwestern American town. One young man works in a junkyard and restricts his sexual activities to rear-end collisions, which is upsetting to his lovely but horny wife. A German emigrant plays out necrophilia fantasies late at night. A female radio evangelist has a peculiar preaching style. The general plot centers on the junkyard worker and his wife.

In contrast to his other ventures into provocative cinema, Meyer builds this film more on sex than on violence. The erotic studies are quite varied, filled with his usual fast cutaways to naked, buxom ladies running inexplicably around the country side.

The film is not without its macabre overtones either. Attempting a comment on prejudice, Meyer has a black laborer bleed white and a gay dentist bleed pink. He titillates, hints, jabs, teases, provokes, shocks, and upsets his audience in such an unusual way that he has become an American institution.

Genre: Erotic
Year: 1979
Time: 86 min.
Acting: Very Good
Casting: Good

Script: Very Good
Production: Good
Directing: Very Good
Theme: Housewives, Strippers
Humor: Yes

BEYOND SHAME ★★

Directors: Fred J. Lincoln and Sharon Mitchell
Cast: Seka, Laurie Blue, Paul Thomas

This film doesn't break any new ground, but it's better than most and full of intense sex scenes.

The plot line is the traditional one concerning a sex therapist and his client (Seka), whose erotic stories are brought to life via flashbacks. Seka's not a bad actress, and she's especially fiery in the erotic encounters. A few lesbian scenes are thrown in for good measure.

This is the sort of film that caters to people who like to watch sexual activity intensely enjoyed, without violence. It was produced and directed by two actors, which is probably why the film's sensuality is so well done.

Genre: Graphic
Year: 1980
Time: 80 min.
Acting: Good
Casting: Fair

Script: Fair
Production: Fair
Directing: Good
Theme: Sex Therapy
Humor: Yes

★ Watchable	★★★ Must See
★★ Recommended	★★★★ Masterpiece

B

BILITIS ★★½

Director: David Hamilton
Cast: Patti d'Arbanville, Mona Kirtensen, Bernard Giraudeau

This is a high-gloss coming-of-age film by photographer David Hamilton, who is noted for his soft-focus photos of erotic women.

Bilitis (Patti d'Arbanville) attends an all-girl school that is about to break for summer. Once on vacation, Bilitis comes to grips with her budding sexuality and strikes up a romantic liaison with a local boy. A secondary romance concerns Bilitis' female guardian and her new husband.

The treatment of sensuality is soft and beautiful, which is in keeping with Hamilton's style of photography. At the beginning of the film, we see the sweet, sensual bodies of the schoolgirls exuberantly bathing in a mountain lake. When Bilitis is finally seduced, it is exaggerated romance, heavily diffused, implying rather than showing their coupling. The lovemaking between the married couple is equally stylized, but more steamy.

The film tries to be honest in portraying Bilitis' coming of age, but often becomes pretentious. Even so, the film continues to be very popular on cable television and in many art theaters.

Genre: Erotic
Year: 1977
Time: 92 min.
Acting: Good
Casting: Good

Script: Fair
Production: Very Good
Directing: Good
Theme: Schoolgirl
Humor: No

BLONDE AMBITION ★★★

Producers/directors: John and Lem Amero
Cast: Suzy Mandel, Dory Devon, Eric Edwards, Jamie Gillis

This delightful comedy attempts some big musical production numbers with very effective results. The women are pretty and have a sense of innocent adventure, making this an exciting film for adult audiences.

Two country blondes meet an Englishman who claims to be a big-time movie agent. The women jump at the chance to go to the big city, but when they get there, they find the Englishman is a phony. Forced to find work, they get involved in a raunchy sex film, and later they land parts in an adult version of *Gone With The Wind*.

As an explicit adult film, this one attempts some new things and does a very fine job.

Genre: Graphic	**Script:** Good
Year: 1980	**Production:** Very Good
Time: 84 min.	**Directing:** Good
Acting: Very Good	**Theme:** Country Girls
Casting: Good	**Humor:** Yes

★	Watchable	★★★	Must See
★★	Recommended	★★★★	Masterpiece

B

BLONDE FIRE ★★

Director: Bob Chinn
Cast: John Holmes, Seka, Jesie St. James, Fay Byrd

Of all the Johnny Wadd (John Holmes) adventure films, this one is without a doubt the best. And although Seka had done a few films before, this one brought her into the limelight.

Johnny Wadd, a tough but very sexy private eye, is hired to bring the Blonde Fire diamond from South Africa to New York. Along the way he outwits the bad guys and gets involved with the ladies. Some of the ladies are after the detective's jewel—but not the one he was born with. That he gives freely and quite generously.

The sex caters to fans who like to see rugged, dominant men and submissive, beautiful women. It contains all the typical adult-formula sex scenes, and its technical execution is extremely high.

Holmes is one of the busiest superstars of the adult film industry, but not because of his acting.

Genre: Graphic
Year: 1979
Time: 96 min.
Acting: Poor
Casting: Fair

Script: Fair
Production: Very Good
Directing: Fair
Theme: Deadly Ladies
Humor: Yes

BLONDE IN BLACK SILK ★★

Director: Philip Drexler Jr.
Cast: Serena, David Bellows, Merle Michaels, Erica Matthews

Another basically standard adult film, but well made, with a lusty, all-out performance by the gorgeous Serena.

Here Serena plays a self-made tycoon who acquires a magazine. She orders some of her reporters to investigate her own affairs, unaware that she's the one who ordered it.

Serena is indefatigable in her sexual exploits, and we're thrust into one erotic encounter after another. These include the traditional lesbian scene, a little bondage, and meetings with motorcycle-gang members.

It's good, strong stuff, but nothing new. Its pluses are the better-than-average photography, the acting, and the overheated Serena.

Genre: Graphic
Year: 1980
Time: 87 min.
Acting: Good
Casting: Fair

Script: Fair
Production: Good
Directing: Good
Theme: Magazine Reporters
Humor: Yes

★ Watchable ★★★ Must See
★★ Recommended ★★★★ Masterpiece

B

THE BLONDE NEXT DOOR

Director: Joe Sherman
Cast: Danielle Martin, Ron Jeremy, Lisa DeLeeuw

Despite its uneven production values and sometimes flawed acting, an abundance of raw creativity makes this film quite entertaining.

The story is about a young blonde, Cindy, who secretes a transparent liquid. A con man, who seduces Cindy, discovers that when other women smell this strange liquid it turns them into sexual animals. He bottles it, and becomes an overnight financial success. The only problem is keeping Cindy erotically stimulated in order to insure his supply—this turns into a major difficulty, as he must think of newer and kinkier ways to arouse her.

Many of the sexual encounters are filled with comic action. The opening scene, where Cindy and her husband make love to a step-by-step recording, is hilariously erotic. The film also makes good use of outdoor sex, lesbianism, group sex, and incest.

A few of the scenes, especially the outdoor ones, are well photographed. But as the film progresses, some of the indoor shots degenerate into poor photography.

Danielle (Cindy) is quite attractive in the lead and has an exquisite sensual personality. Her scene with John Leslie is very erotic.

Genre: Graphic
Year: 1981
Time: 82 min.
Acting: Fair
Casting: Fair

Script: Fair
Production: Good
Directing: Fair
Theme: Hitchhiker
Humor: Yes

BLONDES HAVE MORE FUN   ★★

Director: John Seeman
Cast: Jack Wright, Dorothy LeMay, Seka, Jesie St. James,
John Leslie

While this comedy is certainly not an outstanding film, it is interesting in several aspects.

A near-bankrupt businessman comes across a mad scientist who has discovered a strange potion—a genuine aphrodisiac. One swig and the subject is sent into sexual orbit. Not really thinking it works, the businessman takes a sip and instantly finds himself in a San Francisco cathouse literally exhausting two full-time whores and wearing the madam down to a frazzle. The businessman attempts to market the potion, sending both the plot and the population of California into erotic ecstasy.

The sexual scenes are both explicit and humorous, but too long. This keeps the film from becoming a wacky, far-out, mad scientist spoof.

Few adult films ever attempt anything really creative and fun. At least this one tried. And Seka makes the sex scenes worthwhile.

Genre: Graphic   **Script:** Good
Year: 1981   **Production:** Good
Time: 88 min.   **Directing:** Fair
Acting: Fair   **Theme:** Aphrodisiac
Casting: Fair   **Humor:** Yes

★   Watchable   ★★★   Must See
★★   Recommended   ★★★★ Masterpiece

B

BON APPETIT ★★★

Producer/director: Chuck Vincent
Cast: Kelly Nichols, Gloria Leonard, Randy West

This film boasts many exotic scenes featuring sleek and sexy Kelly Nichols.

A wealthy female publisher makes a wager that she thinks she can positively win. She offers a quarter-million dollars to any woman who can bed the ten best international lovers within a 50-day period. A sexy waitress, fed up with her job, travels to Paris, Rome, Las Vegas, Washington, and Amsterdam in search of the world's top romancers.

The sex scenes are excellently photographed, but move much too quickly and unrealistically. The subtler aspects of seduction have been jettisoned. The film does contain some newly shot European footage—not scenes pulled out of a film library.

Genre: Graphic
Year: 1980
Time: 84 min.
Acting: Good
Casting: Good

Script: Fair
Production: Good
Directing: Very Good
Theme: Waitress
Humor: No

★ Watchable   ★★★ Must See
★★ Recommended   ★★★★ Masterpiece

LESLLIE BOVEE

Lesllie Bovée has been doing adult films since the mid-70's. One of her first ventures was in Alex DeRenzy's S&M classic Femmes de Sade, where she took on a whole gang of hungry sailors.

As legend goes, Lesllie's sensual talents were discovered while she was dancing at The Bucket—a topless bar in Inglewood, California. As an actress, she has developed a reputation as a very sensual, almost trashy, sexual enthusiast. Both William Margold and Mike Ranger have regarded her as one of the top erotic performers in the business, and have greatly enjoyed working with her.

She has starred in Champagne For Breakfast, A Coming of Angels, Eruption, Games Women Play, Misbehavin', Sex World, Take Off, The Ecstasy Girls, Maraschino Cherry, The Erotic Adventures of Pinocchio, and Snow White Comes of Age.

She is currently living in New York where she is writing a book about her very unusual life.

B

THE BUDDING OF BRIE

Director: Henri Pachard
Cast: Hillary Summers, Jennifer Jordan, Eric Edwards

This film started off as just another adult flick, but such care was given to costuming, music, dialogue, and plot that the sex had to take a back seat.

The film is actually a takeoff on the cult classic *All About Eve*. In this version, Brie Livingston is a lowly waitress who becomes an award-winning actress in a single year. She uses her body and sexual charms to scratch her way to power. Victims of her seduction include a top talent agent and several influential film critics.

The problem is this: The sex scenes get in the way and only prolong the film. The sex is explicit, which is not the same as erotic.

Even so, the film has been very popular with audiences and critics and serves as a serious study of sex as a means of getting ahead.

Genre: Graphic	**Script:** Good
Year: 1980	**Production:** Very Good
Time: 88 min.	**Directing:** Very Good
Acting: Good	**Theme:** Casting Couch
Casting: Good	**Humor:** Yes

BUTTERFLIES ★★

Director: Joseph W. Sarno
Cast: Harry Reems, Marie Forsa

Made in Germany, but re-edited for release in the States, this film is wonderfully photographed and performed, with delightful characterizations by Reems and Forsa.

A young, blond farm girl sets out for the big city and lands a job with a nightclub owner (Reems), who eventually becomes her lover. But the girl's desires are just too strong for one man and she finds herself experimenting with other men, which leads to complications.

In the original German version, the sexual encounters were slight and titillated rather than saturated. In the American release, however, some graphic inserts were added, but they're not as excessive as one might think.

With or without the inserts, *Butterflies* is a good example of fine filmmaking and light erotic entertainment. It's fun.

Genre: Graphic
Year: 1974
Time: 93 min.
Acting: Very Good
Casting: Good

Script: Good
Production: Very Good
Directing: Fair
Theme: Country Girl
Humor: Yes

★ Watchable   ★★★ Must See
★★ Recommended   ★★★★ Masterpiece

C

CAFE FLESH

Director: Rinse Dream
Cast: Pia Snow, Kevin Jay, Marie Sharp, Darcy Nycols

This unusual film hasn't yet developed an audience, but in terms of sheer imagery and "bizarreness," it's tops.

A few years after the Big War, in which the world has been brought to near-ruin by a nuclear holocaust, radiation is beginning to have a strange effect on the human libido. People are repulsed by sex and, except for a meager one percent of the population, can't engage in erotic activity at all. The one percent are commissioned by the government to perform in erotic cafes (hence the title). The story is about one such cafe, its strange and exotic clientele, and its wild sex shows.

The shows are both explicit and humorous, the best involving a long-nosed rat that dances around a chorus line of good-looking semi-naked women, poking his proboscis where it doesn't belong.

The emcee is outstanding, and both Pia Snow and Maria Sharp turn in highly charged erotic performances. The acting is heavily stylized and viewers unaccustomed to cultish, avant-garde movies might take offense. This picture is somewhere between an off-beat art film and an adult movie. You'll either love it or hate it.

Genre: Graphic
Year: 1982
Time: 80 min.
Acting: Good
Casting: Good

Script: Very Good
Production: Very Good
Directing: Very Good
Theme: Sex Performers
Humor: Strange

C

CALIGULA ★★

Directors: Bob Guccione and Giancarlo Lui
Cast: Malcolm McDowell, John Gielgud, Peter O'Toole, Helen
Mirren, Teresa Ann Savoy

This was *Penthouse* publisher Bob Guccione's big entry into
adult entertainment. He spent over $30 million on the pro-
duction, which is a shame. This is not that good of a movie.

The film builds around one of the most notoriously decadent of the Roman emperors, Caligula. The movie covers his
rise to power, his four-year rule, and his bloody assassination.
His vile deeds include crashing a wedding and sexually
abusing the bride and groom, playing erotic fantasies with his
sister (who is also his lover) and turning the Imperial Palace
into an exclusive brothel.

For a really big-money film, the treatment of the sexual
scenes is daringly explicit, but somehow the obsession with it
makes the film uneven. It blends very good actors, O'Toole
and McDowell, with some simple-minded *Penthouse* models.
The overall effect is disappointing.

Guccione does deserve a hand for the exquisite sets, cos-
tumes, production values, and very fine cinematography, but
the film is basically a poor man's *Satyricon*.

Genre: Erotic
Year: 1980
Time: 155 min.
Acting: Very Good
Casting: Good

Script: Fair
Production: Very Good
Directing: Poor
Theme: Roman Orgy
Humor: No

★ Watchable	★★★ Must See
★★ Recommended	★★★★ Masterpiece

C

CANDY GOES TO HOLLYWOOD ★★

Producer/director: Gail Palmer
Cast: Carol Connors, John Leslie, Richard Pacheco,
  Phaery Burg

This is the sequel to *The Erotic Adventures of Candy*, a sexy spoof that burst upon the scene in 1978. Both films have excellent production values, lots of sex, and cute stories.

Candy, who was sexually liberated in the original film, now decides to go to Hollywood. She finds that the casting couch is as active as ever, that jiggle is still the status quo in television, and that the producer must always be taken care of first.

The film has the obligatory orgy, replete with swingers, sexy ladies, lesbians, gays, and others. Miss Nude America makes an appearance and Wendy O. Williams, who later became lead singer for the punk group The Plasmatics, does a very explicit scene with a ping-pong ball.

The movie's a lot of fun and the women (especially the well-endowed blonde Carol Connors) are very sexy.

Genre: Graphic
Year: 1979
Time: 88 min.
Acting: Fair
Casting: Good

Script: Fair
Production: Good
Directing: Good
Theme: Casting Couch
Humor: Yes

CANDY STRIPERS ★★★

Director: Bob Chinn
Cast: Amber Hunt, Chris Cassidy (aka Montana),
  Nancy Hoffman, Sharon Thorpe

This sexy hospital comedy features a lot of nice-looking nurses giving patients some exotic therapy. It's wacky, well photographed, and features a healthy dose of medical-fantasy sex.

A sexy nurse who is leaving the hospital plans a final-night going-away party with her two lusty nurse friends. Their prudish supervisor objects, but the nurses are just too irrepressible—it's nurses with patients, nurses with doctors, and, of course, nurses with nurses. Despite today's liberal standards, many scenes were cut from the present available version, but the film loses nothing of its uninhibited erotic quality.

Of all the adult films with hospital settings, this one's the best. It is expertly photographed (Director Chinn's strong point), and the three leading ladies—Hunt, Montana, and Hoffman—help temperatures rise.

Genre: Graphic
Year: 1978
Time: 84 min.
Acting: Good
Casting: Fair

Script: Fair
Production: Very Good
Directing: Good
Theme: Nurses
Humor: Yes

★	Watchable	★★★	Must See
★★	Recommended	★★★★	Masterpiece

C

THE CANTERBURY TALES ★★

Director: Pier Paolo Pasolini
Cast: Pier Paolo Pasolini, Laura Betti, J.P. Van Dyne

This is the second in Pasolini's series of setting classic bawdy tales to film. In this case, he picked eight of Chaucer's *Canterbury Tales,* including the infamous miller's tale and the incident with the red-hot poker kiss.

The tales revolve around a group of pilgrims who are journeying to the shrine of Saint Thomas à Becket of Canterbury. The trip is so tedious that they begin telling each other stories that soon get bawdy, gory and very sexy. Pasolini adds another motif to his visualization by placing Chaucer himself into the film, periodically cutting to him writing at his desk.

Pasolini pokes fun at social customs, especially marriage. Some of the stories are funny, others are deadly serious. The scene where a young man is burned for making love to another of his own sex, for example, is chilling.

The Canterbury Tales, coming right after the popular *Decameron,* was not well received, but has since gained more recognition and popularity. Pasolini dared to show the medieval era as filthy, slummish, vulgar, and riddled with social inequality and hypocrisy. In fact, Pasolini's no-frills approach to filmmaking, using non-professional actors, is more in keeping with the tone of the original than the usual romanticized versions.

Genre: Erotic
Year: 1972
Time: 109 min.
Acting: Very Good
Casting: Excellent

Script: Good
Production: Fair
Directing: Very Good
Theme: Strumpets
Humor: Yes

CENTERFOLD FEVER ★★

Producer/director: Richard Milner
Cast: Samantha Fox, Colette Connor, Marc Stevens,
   Annie Sprinkle

This is a "men's magazine" film, but a very good one. It was produced and directed by the managing editor of a bona fide girlie magazine, but the film is more of an adult male fantasy about the skin-magazine business.

The publisher of a sleazy nudie magazine keeps coming up empty-handed in his quest for the perfect centerfold girl. Then suddenly, one of his female reporters happens by a swinging New York party and finds the nastiest, most erotic, lusty, beautiful woman she's ever seen. The only problem— she doesn't want to be photographed.

Centerfold Girls isn't a realistic film, but it does feature a lot of good-looking, model-type girls in extremely compromising situations. The sex is indulgent, graphic, fun, and full of variation.

It's a flippant, well-made adult comedy that's been underrated by many critics.

Genre: Graphic	**Script:** Fair
Year: 1981	**Production:** Good
Time: 80 min.	**Directing:** Fair
Acting: Good	**Theme:** Nude Models
Casting: Good	**Humor:** Yes

★ Watchable	★★★ Must See
★★ Recommended	★★★★ Masterpiece

C

CENTERSPREAD GIRLS ★★

Producer: Harold Lime
Director: Robert McCallum
Cast: Annette Haven, Veronica Hart, Jesie St. James

Another "men's magazine" comedy which, like *Centerfold Fever*, is richly produced and full of exuberant, pretty girls.

To combat a group of religious zealots hounding her nudie magazine, a female publisher calls on several former centerspread models to seduce some of them. Photographs are then taken of these sessions.

The girls get the zealots into some wild positions that are sexy as well. Viewers who like a lot of sex on screen will certainly have their prayers answered—however, the graphic sex here is not for the faint-hearted.

Producer Harold Lime is noted for high production values and this film is no exception. His films are always entertaining, generally inoffensive, and sizzlingly erotic.

Genre: Graphic
Year: 1982
Time: 95 min.
Acting: Fair
Casting: Good

Script: Fair
Production: Good
Directing: Fair
Theme: Nude Models
Humor: Yes

★ Watchable ★★★ Must See
★★ Recommended ★★★★ Masterpiece

MARILYN CHAMBERS

When first approached by the Mitchell brothers, Marilyn Chambers refused to do adult films. She later changed her mind and accepted a role in Behind the Green Door, which catapulted her into stardom. She was one of the first elegant, pretty women to do an explicit adult film. In fact, she had had a brief career as a model, appearing on the Ivory Snow detergent box—hence the term, "The Ivory Snow Girl."

Ms. Chambers has not done that many adult films. She has built her reputation on four films alone: Behind the Green Door, The Resurrection of Eve, Inside Marilyn Chambers (a documentary), and Insatiable. She is one of the few actresses in the adult-film business to have captured leading roles in other genres, most notably the much promoted horror film Rabid and the racy stage play The Sex Surrogate.

Her lover/manager is Linda Lovelace's ex-boyfriend/manager, Chuck Traynor, whom she says is a sweet, gentle man. Chambers plans to continue doing both adult and general-interest films.

C

CHAMPAGNE FOR BREAKFAST

Director: Billy Thornberg
Cast: Lesllie Bovèe, John Leslie, Kay Parker, Kandi Barbour

This is a pearl of erotic filmmaking. In it, veterans Lesllie Bovèe and John Leslie give fine performances. It has solid photography, superior acting, and some very interesting scenes.

Champagne, played by Lesllie Bovèe, is a young, ambitious career woman who has just landed a big promotion in a cosmetic company. Her female co-executives show her how to manipulate success-oriented male underlings into erotic encounters, but she wants more out of her sex life. She doesn't quite know what this "something" is and embarks on a sensual journey to find out.

Champagne indulges in quite a rich variety of sexual situations, looking for that "something." Despite the number of men she uses, however, she never seems to find it. The sex scenes logically grow out of the plot, and the one in the car wash is particularly hilarious.

On the whole, this film combines comedy and sex with posh settings. A very fine erotic farce, one of the best of recent years.

Genre: Graphic
Year: 1980
Time: 102 min.
Acting: Very Good
Casting: Good

Script: Good
Production: Very Good
Directing: Good
Theme: Woman Corporate Executive
Humor: Yes

C

CHARLI ★★

Producer/director: Godfrey Daniels
Cast: Jesie St. James, Eric Edwards, Annette Haven, Billy Dee

This is one of the first of recent films geared toward female audiences. It's more sympathetic to female, rather than male, fantasies and avoids offensiveness in its sexual encounters.

A young couple whose sexual fire for each other is dimming try fantasizing about extra-marital sex. However, unlike most adult films—where characters seem to jump into bed with the first person they see—*Charli* takes its time. Characters select partners, get to know them, and the lovemaking builds to a climax. The husband even admits a lack of sensitivity and apologizes to his wife—which won't sit well with some rough and tumble male viewers.

The sex is tender, dynamic, and very explicit. Although its music and some technical aspects aren't well polished, it certainly has a chance of appealing to those unsatisfied with the usual themes of adult-oriented films.

Genre: Graphic
Year: 1981
Time: 78 min.
Acting: Good
Casting: Good

Script: Good
Production: Fair
Directing: Good
Theme: Housewife
Humor: No

★ Watchable ★★★ Must See
★★ Recommended ★★★★ Masterpiece

C

CHERRY, HARRY AND RAQUEL

Director: Russ Meyer
Cast: Larissa Ely, Linda Ashton, Charles Napier

Like *Supervixens, Cherry, Harry and Raquel* is a swiftly paced excursion into sex and violence.

The story takes place in the Nevada desert. Mr. Franklin is a prominent man in the community who also happens to run a drug-smuggling ring on the side. The local sheriff is in on it, acting as Mr. Franklin's hit man. After a hot scene with one of the local wenches, Mr. Franklin orders the sheriff to eliminate the Apache, an Indian who has been cutting into their marijuana sales. The sheriff reluctantly agrees, takes the boss's woman home, and vents his frustrations on her before trying to blow the Indian away.

Meyer does indeed have a fascination for very richly endowed women, and this film is no exception. The scene where Franklin talks the nurse into giving him a body massage is a classic erotic tease. Also, Meyer has very deftly juxtaposed a sensual lesbian scene against a bloody battle between the sheriff and the Indian. But much of the sex is unmotivated. Meyer cuts so quickly, however, that it is more of a flippant tease than an exploitive treatment of sex.

Despite some high-strung acting, many of the characterizations border on caricature. But Larissa Ely is wonderful as the seedy, steamy, sweaty desert lass. Linda Ashton is delightful as the sexy nurse, but Charles Napier steals the show as the explosive, cartoonish, tyrant of a sheriff.

Genre: Erotic	**Script:** Fair
Year: 1969	**Production:** Good
Time: 71 min.	**Directing:** Good
Acting: Good	**Theme:** Nurses
Casting: Very Good	**Humor:** Yes

CHINA DE SADE ★

Director: Charles DeSantos
Cast: Linda Wong, Tracy O'Neil, Kelly O'Day

This tongue-in-cheek ode to sex and sadism is a little too silly for its own good, thanks to the makers' ineptitude. However, the performers seem to enjoy what they're doing, including the torture.

A mysterious government agency assigns one of its agents to infiltrate a U.S. organization involved in a Chinese agent's defection. He does, and is caught up in a sex/torture ring.

The movie is fraught with bondage, rape, raw lust, and raunchy sex. None of it can be taken seriously because the situations are so preposterous. It does try to turn many of the forced sex situations into willing game-playing episodes, with only lukewarm results.

Oddly, the movie is so off-the-wall and the sex so out of place that it's somewhat humorous, even appealing. Definitely unappealing are the lighting, sound, and editing, which are practically nil.

Genre: Graphic
Year: 1979
Time: 80 min.
Acting: Poor
Casting: Fair

Script: Poor
Production: Fair
Directing: Fair
Theme: Torture
Humor: No

★ Watchable ★★★ Must See
★★ Recommended ★★★★ Masterpiece

C

CHORUS CALL ★★

Director: Antonio Sheppard
Cast: Kay Parker, Darby Lloyd Rains, Beth Anna,
Susan London

This erotic takeoff on the musical *Chorus Line* may not be original, but it does have a lot of gusto and sexual energy.

The story follows the original quite closely, but delves more into the sexual antics of getting into show business. The play's the thing, of course—how it's produced, cast, and performed, and the fact that the leading lady has the final say as to who gets into the production. Naturally, she's interested in more than just one's singing and dancing ability.

There is a lot of sex and most of it is heavy and fun. Two lesbian episodes are particularly hilarious.

The music is much better than in most low-budget pictures, and some optical effects have interesting results. Kay Parker is excellent as a crusty, lusty matron of the theater.

The movie is entertaining, very erotic, and above average in its production value.

Genre: Graphic
Year: 1978
Time: 78 min.
Acting: Good
Casting: Fair

Script: Fair
Production: Good
Directing: Fair
Theme: Casting Couch
Humor: Yes

CITY OF WOMEN ★★★★

Director: Federico Fellini
Cast: Marcello Mastroianni, Ettore Manni, Bernice Stegers, Donatella Damiani

Of all the Fellini films, this is probably his most erotic. It is not as much a study of eroticism as it is one man's erotic fantasy about the battle between the sexes.

A rich, horny Italian (Mastroianni) meets a woman on a train. When the train stops, he follows her into a lonely wood, which becomes a futuristic world of aggressive women who have virtually annihilated all men in their society. Mastroianni's character is left alive as a curiosity piece. His experiences carry him deeper and deeper into this bizarre fantasy city.

The film never fully caters to flippant erotic lusts, but is titillating and stimulating none the less. Fellini's point—that women resent the fact that men are easily aroused—is most effectively conveyed by Damiani, a buxom and very beautiful young actress who runs nearly naked throughout the movie.

Although the film never tires, it never quite fulfills its erotic expectations either, preferring instead to explore its own bizarre reality. It has elements of science fiction and adventure, but is more exactly a fantasy on the estrangement between men and women.

Genre: Erotic	**Script:** Excellent
Year: 1981	**Production:** Excellent
Time: 138 min.	**Directing:** Excellent
Acting: Very Good	**Theme:** Science Fiction
Casting: Very Good	**Humor:** Yes

★ Watchable ★★★ Must See
★★ Recommended ★★★★ Masterpiece

C

CLOCKWORK ORANGE

Director: Stanley Kubrick
Cast: Malcolm McDowell, Patrick Magee, Michael Bates, Warren Clarke

Like Fellini's *City of Women*, this film was not made to cater to audiences of erotic films, but used blatant sexual and violent devices to make its point. When it first came out, the sex and violence were graphic enough to earn an X-rating. Soon after, it was re-edited to an R.

The story is a parable of the future, tracing the rise and fall and rise again of Alex—a violent rapist. Alex becomes a guinea pig for a Pavlovian conditioning experiment that supposedly turns criminals into "good" citizens. Critics of the treatment say it takes away the freedom of choice, which is what good and bad is all about anyway. After the conditioning, the two things that Alex has always enjoyed, sex and violence, now make him extremely sick. When he re-enters society, instead of being the aggressor, he becomes the victim.

The film was one of the first mainstream, serious films to show some extremely graphic rape scenes. And throughout the film, we are repeatedly bombarded by sexual images.

Clockwork Orange is a unique film, a masterful excursion into the world of sex and violence.

Genre: Taboo
Year: 1971
Time: 137 min.
Acting: Very Good
Casting: Excellent

Script: Excellent
Production: Excellent
Directing: Excellent
Theme: Rape
Humor: Some

COED FEVER ★★

Director: Robert McCallum
Cast: Annette Haven, Samantha Fox, Brooke West, Serena

With the success of *Animal House*, a rash of fraternity house
adult films hit the market. Of the lot, *Coed Fever* is one of the
best.

A sorority house, whose president is the sleek Annette
Haven, is chosen to be the feature article of a big national
magazine, and Annette tries to clean up her girls' manners.
The lusty young ladies, however, have ideas of their own, and
conspire with their fraternity buddies to sabotage the big day.

The sex is big, insane, and delightful. The romp of the
prudish Annette as she is being ecstatically "abused" by one
of the boys under a table is one of the greatest-ever erotic
scenes. Another great scene is the sorority's spanking initiation ritual. Samantha Fox and Vanessa Del Rio are scintillat-
ing throughout.

The film is a clever trip into a sophomoric, collegiate fantasy. Robert McCallum is a fine technical director, but often
has trouble getting good performances from his cast. In this
film, he does a better-than-usual job.

Genre: Graphic
Year: 1980
Time: 90 min.
Acting: Fair
Casting: Good

Script: Fair
Production: Good
Directing: Fair
Theme: College Girls
Humor: Yes

★ Watchable   ★★★ Must See
★★ Recommended   ★★★★ Masterpiece

C

COMING ATTRACTIONS ★★

Director: Duncan Starr
Cast: Sharon Thorpe, John Leslie, Desiree West, Al Poe,
Benny Moore

Also titled *Sex Drive*, this small gem of a movie wasn't well
made but still comes off as quite entertaining.

A young couple, Sharon Thorpe and John Leslie, are traveling down Interstate 15 to Las Vegas. During the trip, the film
takes us in and out of both characters' erotic fantasies. The
woman dreams about having an affair with a service station
attendant, for example, and John Leslie conjures up one of his
old girlfriends while his wife is taking a shower in a motel
room. And so it goes, in and out of these daydreams.

While the technical aspects are standard, low-key, and uninspired, the sexual encounters are vibrant, exciting, and
really make the film work. It moves swiftly from scene to
scene, keeping the audience strangely offguard.

As an adult film, it is delightful to watch—especially the
young John Leslie. This was one of his first films, and in it he
exudes a youthful, innocent charm.

Genre: Graphic	**Script:** Good
Year: 1976	**Production:** Fair
Time: 75 min.	**Directing:** Fair
Acting: Good	**Theme:** Erotic Fantasies
Casting: Good	**Humor:** Yes

A COMING OF ANGELS ★★

Producer/director: Joel Scott
Cast: Lesllie Bovèe, Abigail Clayton, Annette Haven,
   Amber Hunt, Jamie Gillis

This film takes the same premise as *Charlie's Angels* —
great-looking women, silly detective stories, innocent sexy
teasing—and pushes the erotic tease part a little further. The
result is a superb, light sexual comedy.

A very good-looking female private eye is kidnapped by a
gang, and her two private-eye girlfriends try to rescue her.
That's all, folks.

The sex scenes are sometimes soft and tender, other times
rugged and heavy. While the three-way lesbian scene runs
way too long, it is nonetheless an exceptional one. The
women are always enthusiastic, pretty, and very stimulating.
Annette Haven and Abigail Clayton are two of the most
gorgeous-looking women in adult films, and Lesllie Bovèe is
certainly one of the most erotic.

In the 1978 Erotica Award Ceremony, this film copped three
awards for acting. The story is silly, often indulgent, sometimes slow, but entertaining overall.

Genre: Graphic
Year: 1977
Time: 87 min.
Acting: Good
Casting: Good

Script: Fair
Production: Good
Directing: Good
Theme: Female Private Eyes
Humor: Yes

★ Watchable   ★★★ Must See
★★ Recommended   ★★★★ Masterpiece

CAROL CONNORS

Carol Connors may play the dumb blonde in her films, but she's a very shrewd business-oriented woman in real life. She made her first appearance in the famed Deep Throat as the kooky doctor's nurse but her appearance has changed remarkably since then. The new Carol is much more elegant, striking, and sexy.

She is most noted for her Candy roles in The Erotic Adventures of Candy and Candy Goes to Hollywood, but has appeared in a number of other films including Sweet Savage, Road of Death, School Teacher's Weekend Vacation, and Water People.

She has recently directed herself in the new Mitchell Brothers release Desire For Men, which reveals some rather kinky aspects of her sexual fantasies.

DESIREE COUSTEAU   *aka Desiree Clearbranch*

Many performers have different on- and offscreen personalities. But Desiree Cousteau is very much the woman one sees in the movies. She is sweet, adorably naive, dizzy, and vibrantly full of life.

Like Annette Haven, she was discovered by the director Alex DeRenzy, who cast this lovely young woman in a leading role despite her total lack of film experience. The film was Pretty Peaches, and her role was so popular that the AFAA (Adult Film Association of America) awarded her Best Actress for the year 1977.

While she has only really portrayed a single type of woman, she has been in quite a number of adult films including Candy Goes to Hollywood, Easy, The Ecstasy Girls, 800 Fantasy Lane, Ms. Magnificent, Randy, The Electric Lady, Centerspread Girls and The Hot and Saucy Pizza Girls.

C

CRY UNCLE

Director: John G. Avildsen
Cast: Allen Garfield, Madeline Le Roux, Devin Goldenberg

A very amusing, tightly directed spoof of the old murder-mystery formula.

Jake Masters, a pot-bellied, not-very-good-looking private eye is hired by a wealthy man who is the prime suspect in the murder of a young starlet. It is Jake's job to find the real murderer. He not only uncovers the case, but also a lot of hookers and call girls.

The misadventures are hilarious and include coitus interruptus, unintentional necrophilia, and sinister lesbians. The sexual overtones are titillating and funny. They are used more to comment on the hypocrisy of society than to exploit.

There is a lot of soul in this film, especially in the performance of Allen Garfield (Masters), who plays a very adorable investigator. Madeline Le Roux is volcanic as the fiery blond who is as quick with a pistol as she is with her verbal assaults.

John Avildsen went on to direct the box-office smash *Rocky*.

Genre: Erotic
Year: 1971
Time: 90 min.
Acting: Very Good
Casting: Excellent

Script: Very Good
Production: Very Good
Directing: Very Good
Theme: Starlets, Hookers
Humor: Yes

DAMIANO'S PEOPLE ★

Director: Gerard Damiano
Cast: Serena, Samantha Fox, Marlene Willoughby,
    Jamie Gillis, Richard Bolla

A series of short subjects whose only unifying thread is the director, Gerard Damiano—a pioneer in adult entertainment. It is one of the better examples of this kind of filmmaking, which, by its very nature, usually does not lend itself to a cohesive whole.

It is broken into six parts. The first is a mild bondage scene between Jamie Gillis and Serena (who, in real life, have been lovers). The most exciting episode is the third one, where a number of virile young men are set upon by voluptuous female vampires. The other segments are pretty much standard adult situations, except for a cameo appearance by Damiano himself.

As usual, Damiano's feeling for eroticism is mingled with off-beat, occasionally effective humor, and ultra-dirty situations. He's a solid craftsman in the adult underground.

Genre: Graphic
Year: 1979
Time: 76 min.
Acting: Good
Casting: Good

Script: Poor
Production: Fair
Directing: Fair
Theme: Sex Film Stars
Humor: Yes

★ Watchable ★★★ Must See
★★ Recommended ★★★★ Masterpiece

D

THE DANCERS ★★★

Director: Anthony Spinelli
Cast: John Leslie, Kay Parker, Randy West, Mai Lin

Exotic male dancers performing before an all-female audience has proven to be a bonanza for nightclub owners. *The Dancers* is a film about this fad and is quite nicely done.

The action begins when The Dreams, an exotic male dancing team, arrive in a small, midwestern town. It doesn't take long before the women of the hamlet flock to the North Point Saloon, where the show is to take place. The movie soon becomes an erotic tangle as the ladies can't get enough of the boys.

The sex scenes grow organically out of their situations and will certainly appeal to the growing female audience for adult entertainment. The production values are superior, though uneven at times. The intensity, however, remains high throughout.

The screenplay was voted best of 1981 by the Adult Film Association of America.

Genre: Graphic
Year: 1981
Time: 97 min.
Acting: Very Good
Casting: Good

Script: Very Good
Production: Very Good
Directing: Good
Theme: Male Exotic Dancers
Humor: Yes

DEBBIE DOES DALLAS ★

Director: Jim Clark
Cast: Bambi Wood, Richard Bolla, Eric Edwards, Misty
  Winter, Merle Michaels

From an acting and technical point of view, this film is not
very good, yet it has done phenomenally well at the box office. Over the last three years, it has been one of the best adult
videocassette sellers as well.

The film was made during the controversy over the Dallas
Cowboy cheerleaders doing a pictorial in Playboy. The girls
maintained they were encouraged by the football people, the
football people say no.

Then along comes a film that supposedly stars one of the
cheerleaders. (Actually, Bambi Woods tried out for the squad,
but never made it.) The movie made it, and big. In it, the girls
try to raise money for the "Texas Cowgirl" cheerleading
squad, and find that the task is much easier when they turn on
their womenly charms.

The film contains an abundance of varied and energy-
packed sexual encounters, and near the end, Bambi Woods
gives a superb performance. Still, except for the cheerleading
premise and its remarkable popularity, the film has little to
offer.

Genre: Graphic
Year: 1978
Time: 80 min.
Acting: Poor
Casting: Fair

Script: Poor
Production: Fair
Directing: Poor
Theme: Cheerleaders
Humor: Yes

★ Watchable   ★★★ Must See
★★ Recommended   ★★★★ Masterpiece

D

THE DECAMERON ★★★

Director: Pier Paolo Pasolini
Cast: Franco Citti, Ninetto Davoli, Angela Luce

This is the first of Pasolini's three feature-film adaptations of bawdy tales of antiquity, the other two being *The Canterbury Tales* and *The Arabian Nights*. *The Decameron* is lively, gutsy, and quite funny, well deserving of a superior rating despite its uneven cinematography.

The film contains ten of Boccaccio's most famous tales. The bawdiest story concerns a merchant who "back-doors" his partner's wife by promising to tell her his secret of turning a woman to a mare and back to a woman again.

The tale of the two lovers sleeping together on the terrace is quite nice and very erotic, but the most hilarious one involves a young man who pretends he's a deaf mute in order to get into a convent. Once inside, he discovers that the sisters are very curious about all the fuss the world has made over sex and want to find out if it is worth it.

The stories are quite funny and the acting is adequate— especially for non-professionals. But the film's charm is in its raw energy. It spends as much time showing nude men as it does showing nude women, which was quite unusual for its time.

Genre: Erotic
Year: 1970
Time: 110 min.
Acting: Good
Casting: Very Good

Script: Good
Production: Fair
Directing: Very Good
Theme: Nuns
Humor: Yes

DEEP INSIDE ANNIE SPRINKLE ★★

Director: Annie Sprinkle
Cast: Annie Sprinkle, Judy Bilodeau, Mal O'Ree, Lisa Be

Of all the "inside," pseudo-documentary life stories of sex stars, this is probably the kinkiest. Annie Sprinkle is one of the most insatiable, deviant, noisiest, sexual hobbyists around. And her movie, which might be much closer to reality than one might think, shows why.

The very voluptuous Annie tells her life story in episodes that are re-created and undoubtedly exaggerated to make them more appealing. Her philosophy of eroticism is basically "anything goes."

One of the most sensual scenes is a seven-girl pajama party when Annie was a little girl. Another episode occurs in a sleazy theater where she gets it on with an exclusive, all-male audience.

For those who like deviant—and we mean deviant!—sex, this is the film to see. It's got just about everything, and it's done with above-average acting and production values, making this film a classic of its kind.

Genre: Graphic	**Script:** Poor
Year: 1981	**Production:** Good
Time: 87 min.	**Directing:** Fair
Acting: Fair	**Theme:** Annie Sprinkle
Casting: Good	**Humor:** No

★	Watchable	★★★	Must See
★★	Recommended	★★★★	Masterpiece

D

DEEP THROAT   ★★

Director: Gerard Damiano
Cast: Linda Lovelace, Harry Reems, Dolly Sharp,
  Carol Connors, William Love

Deep Throat is basically a bad movie, really bad. The lighting
is poor, the acting terrible, the directing nonexistent, the
editing inept, and the story is so silly that no one can take it
seriously. Yet, it is probably the best-known erotic underground film ever.

The story concerns a woman who discovers that her clitoris
is in her throat. She finds this out from a very kooky doctor,
played by Harry Reems, who also tells her that the only way to
find erotic happiness is through oral sex.

Despite its crude style, there is something embarrassingly
attractive about this film. The reason for its success is simple
—it was the first film to combine graphic sex with off-the-wall
humor. This formula was so successful that adult features still
copy it today.

Genre: Graphic	**Script:** Poor
Year: 1972	**Production:** Poor
Time: 62 min.	**Directing:** Poor
Acting: Poor	**Theme:** Nurses
Casting: Fair	**Humor:** Yes

DEFIANCE ★

Director: Armond Weston
Cast: Jean Jennings, Fred Lincoln

This extremely uneven movie tries blending various themes that don't mix.

Jean Jennings plays a young girl sent to a mental institution for observation. There she is abused, raped and humiliated, and finally introduced to a bondage cult—a ritualized world of whips and chains.

The sex is awkward and often interferes with the story. Once Ms. Jennings is in erotic situations, however, she is quite energetic. The general theme of the sexual union is force. Jennings is forced to have sex with an orderly, with lesbian inmates, and with a gang of psychos. The last third of the film in the cult temple is almost one constant orgy.

Jean Jennings is cute and innocent with a perky, youthful face. She is very convincing as a young girl, and her reaction for most situations is accurate despite the illogic—especially the ending, which is inept.

Genre: Graphic
Year: 1974
Time: 90 min.
Acting: Fair
Casting: Fair

Script: Poor
Production: Fair
Directing: Poor
Theme: Bondage, Hospital Patient
Humor: No

★ Watchable   ★★★ Must See
★★ Recommended   ★★★★ Masterpiece

D

LISA DeLEEUW

Lisa was born and raised in the Midwest, and moved some years ago to the Los Angeles area, where she became involved in films. Her potent sexuality and free life-style quickly led her into erotic films, where she took off like fire in dry grass.

Behind the camera, Lisa is sweet, almost shy. But once she gets in front of a camera—an audience—she is transformed into a charismatic, powerful, sexy young lady. She has not been extremely versatile as an actress, usually playing the tough, aggressive female who knows how to handle a man.

She is one of the few attractive big-busted actresses in the industry, and has a healthy crop of bright red hair. Her most flamboyant films are 8 to 4; Garage Girls; The Blonde Next Door; Skintight; Downstairs/Upstairs; Plato's, The Movie; Frat House; Coed Fever; Pink Champagne; Nanci Blue; Amanda By Night; and The Filthy Rich.

DELICIOUS ★★★

Director: Philip Drexler Jr.
Cast: Veronica Hart, Candida Royalle, Aaron Stuart

A delightful, supernatural film with some interesting special effects. It's fresh, creative, and very entertaining.

A super-rich family hires a maid who's actually a witch—a sort of supernatural servant with incredible powers over sex. She quickly turns the household into a frenzy of erotic experimentation.

The story moves swiftly with many special effects—nothing elaborate, but quite effective for such a low-budget film. One interesting scene involves the maid turning herself and the lady of the house into miniature people on a note pad. They find that the crayons and pencils are suddenly as large as they are, and use the new-found equipment for erotic experiments. In another scene, the maid enters a room and creates a mysterious wind that blows off everybody's clothes.

The sex scenes are surprisingly organic to the plot and characters and, except for an occasional lapse into uneventful lovemaking, they generally keep the plot moving quickly.

The film is an exuberant sex comedy that should have a large following among both men and women.

Genre: Graphic
Year: 1981
Time: 85 min.
Acting: Very Good
Casting: Good

Script: Good
Production: Very Good
Directing: Very Good
Theme: Maid
Humor: Yes

★ Watchable ★★★ Must See
★★ Recommended ★★★★ Masterpiece

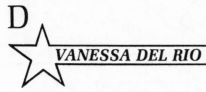

D

VANESSA DEL RIO

This hot-blooded, large-breasted, Cuban dynamo is noted as one of the most insatiable actresses in the adult film business. On screen, she gives a genuine impression that she thoroughly enjoys what she is doing. Her delight in kinky and off-beat sexual games is matched by her incredible energy.

Unlike a number of other adult film stars, Vanessa has no intentions of doing anything other than what she is currently doing. She was raised in New York City and continues to live there.

Outside the adult film business, she also dances in many of the hedonistic clubs and occasionally goes on a burlesque tour.

Vanessa has appeared in quite a number of erotic films, some of the better ones being: Afternoon Delights, Babylon Pink, Justine, Odyssey, Pink Ladies, Scent of Heather, The Filthy Rich, Foxtrot, and The Dancers.

DESIRE FOR MEN ★★

Director: Carol Connors
Cast: Carol Connors, Long Jean Silver, Hershel Savage

The star of the Candy Stories, Carol Connors, turns to directing, although her real gift remains in portraying brainless, chesty blondes in pursuit of sexual delights. This is a strange, unsettling film that moves quite carelessly between eroticism and perversion.

It is about a mother and her daughter. Outwardly, the mother is very prim and proper, but harbors some lewd secret vices. One day the daughter, who has been brought up a "good" girl, is shocked to find her mother with one of her secret lovers. She runs off to discover her own sexuality and ends up spiraling downward into increasingly deviant sexual thrills.

The movie first portrays sex in a lusty, erotic way. But be warned: it quickly moves toward some really weird stuff that becomes anti-erotic, even sickening. The film's strong point is the beginning, when Carol is an innocent, sweet-looking girl entering her first sexual experiences.

Genre: Graphic
Year: 1981
Time: 75 min.
Acting: Fair
Casting: Fair

Script: Poor
Production: Good
Directing: Fair
Theme: Virgin
Humor: No

★ Watchable   ★★★ Must See
★★ Recommended   ★★★★ Masterpiece

D

DESIRES WITHIN YOUNG GIRLS

Director: Ramsey Karason
Cast: Georgina Spelvin, Annette Haven, Clair Dia, Abigail
  Clayton

Annette Haven and Clair Dia are cast as a couple of adolescent
girls right out of school, but both look five years too old. Also,
while Annette's performance is marvelous, Clair Dia's is
stilted and dull. Good thing the sex is great.

Georgina Spelvin adeptly plays an aging widow who feels
her womanly charms are on the decline. To maintain her life-
style, she introduces her daughters to some wealthy friends in
the hope of marrying them off. But, the girls have romantic
ideas of their own.

Despite the dearth of erotic buildup in most scenes, many
are very well-crafted and executed with enthusiasm. There is
lesbianism, a touch of school girl fetishes, ménage à trois,
dominant females, leather, sex in a shower, and some comedic
S & M. Annette Haven handles it all with a classic Fanny Hill
approach. She's beautiful, perky, energetic, and smart. After a
while we begin to believe, despite her older looks, that she is a
schoolgirl.

Well-photographed and directed, this film helped adult
movies move from dreary, pessimistic stories into delightful,
cheery homages to eroticism. A classic.

Genre: Graphic
Year: 1977
Time: 97 min.
Acting: Very Good
Casting: Good

Script: Good
Production: Very Good
Directing: Very Good
Theme: Young Girls
Humor: Yes

DESPERATE LIVING ★★

Director: John Waters
Cast: Liz Renay, Mink Stole, Edith Massey

Desperate filmmaking is more like it. This movie is raw, crude, and only mildly less offensive than John Waters's first excursion into repellent visuals, *Pink Flamingos*.

A screaming, insane housewife accidentally kills her husband by having a 250-pound nurse sit on his face. Fugitives from justice, she and the nurse go on the lam, ending up in the town of Mortville. They fall into a very strange social structure where a perversely ugly queen rules. The town is populated with degenerates, outcasts, and fellow fugitives. There, the women try to carve out a living.

John Waters will not go down in history as a subtle filmmaker. He bludgeons his way through an extraordinary amount of gutter jokes, high-strung acting, perversions, and diatribes. He uses erotica for shock only and for showing people at their worst.

If you like vomit, ugly people, and sexual perversions, Waters is your man.

Genre: Taboo
Year: 1977
Time: 88 min.
Acting: Fair
Casting: Excellent

Script: Fair
Production: Poor
Directing: Very Good
Theme: Housewives, usually mad
Humor: Yes

★ Watchable   ★★★ Must See
★★ Recommended   ★★★★ Masterpiece

D

DEVIL IN MISS JONES ★★★★

Director: Gerard Damiano
Cast: Georgina Spelvin, John Clemens, Harry Reems,
Marc Stevens, Rick Livermore

Since making *Deep Throat*, Gerard Damiano must have
learned a thing or two about filmmaking. This one is a gem.

After committing suicide to escape her dreary, uneventful
life, an aging woman has an interview with a mysterious man
in the afterworld. If she had her life to live over, she says,
she'd do it consumed with lust. The man grants her wish, and
she is ushered into another room.

There, she meets an erotic mentor (Harry Reems), who in-
structs her in the art of making love. She is carried through a
number of very intense sex scenes, and changes from a
prudish spinster into a foul-mouthed, sex-crazed vixen.

The film was Georgina's stunning debut in adult films, and
she demonstrates a remarkable aptitude for acting as well as
for eroticism. The film was also the first successful serious
feature to use some good photography, lighting, and camera
techniques with explicit sex. The existential ending may be
shocking.

Genre: Graphic
Year: 1972
Time: 68 min.
Acting: Good
Casting: Very Good

Script: Very Good
Production: Excellent
Directing: Excellent
Theme: Virgin, Afterlife
Humor: No

D

DEVIL'S ECSTASY   ★★

Director: Brandon G. Carter
Cast: Deborah Whitney, Tara Blair, John McKnight, David
  Lamont, Debbie Garland

One of the few adult films to attempt a story about the occult,
it effectively combines mystery, the supernatural, and eroticism.

A girl fails to return after going off to visit her long-lost
aunt. Her boyfriend goes looking for her, only to enter a
strange world of sensual fanatics and Satan worshippers. The
environment becomes so cloudy that it's hard to tell what's
reality and what's fantasy. Symbolism is rampant—especially
the use of the tarot-card images—and the sex scenes are
crafted with such unusual technique that the audience is almost constantly kept off-balance.

The sexual encounters are highly ritualized, sometimes
pretentious, sometimes quite erotic, but always explicit and
intense. The movie is filled with mood lighting, strange settings, and dark images.

As an erotic occult film, it works well. It is probably the best
of its kind in the adult-entertainment business.

Genre: Graphic	**Script:** Fair
Year: 1974	**Production:** Good
Time: 76 min.	**Directing:** Fair
Acting: Fair	**Theme:** Witches
Casting: Fair	**Humor:** No

★	Watchable	★★★	Must See
★★	Recommended	★★★★	Masterpiece

D

A DIRTY WESTERN   ★

Director: David Fleetwood
Cast: Barbara Bourbon, Richard O'Neal, Levi Richards

This is one of few adult westerns. Three convicts escape from prison and stumble across a ranch. The ranchers have gone on a four-day cattle drive, leaving only the women—a mother and three daughters—to tend the farm. The cons proceed to rape the women.

Except for the opening sexual encounter between the ranch woman and her husband, the sex is brutal, aggressive, and harsh. The girls spend most of the time moaning and crying, the men shouting. The film is very much exploitative in nature and doesn't attempt anything new or different. The convicts are bad guys, the girls innocent victims, and the posse hard-working country types.

The girls are too old to be convincing, and their acting is often downright poor. Bourbon, however, is genuine as a woman being terrorized by a gang of brutal cons.

The cinematography is quite effective in capturing the lush wilderness. And some of the underwater shots are exceptional.

Genre: Graphic   **Script:** Fair
Year: 1975   **Production:** Good
Time: 75 min.   **Directing:** Fair
Acting: Fair   **Theme:** Rape
Casting: Fair   **Humor:** No

DIVINE

While John Waters was a student of film in Baltimore, he used to notice a heavily painted transvestite wandering around the downtown area. When he began making his exotically perverted films, she/he was one of his first casting choices.

Of all the stock actors in Waters's films, Divine is perhaps the one with the liveliest spark for genuine acting talent. She/he does bring out some very intense, high-strung dramatic sequences, and has a remarkable ability to carry an entire movie despite his/her absolutely repulsive physical attributes. One of Divine's most powerful scenes is in Female Trouble where she/he is executed in the electric chair. She/he sings and dances with glee and abandon moments before the switch is pulled. Unlike the other members of the cast, Divine gives us a sense that in some odd, sinister way, this is really happening to her/him. Other performers give the impression that they are just play acting.

Of course, Divine's most famous scene is the coprophagy at the end of Pink Flamingos. She is obviously not enjoying the incident, but forces a smile anyway.

Divine has recently appeared in Waters's newest excursion into sleaze and camp in the film Polyester, where she/he plays a frustrated suburban housewife.

Divine grew up in a middle-class Maryland suburban home, and his/her real name is Glenn. How she/he went from that to starring in Waters's films may very well be another story, worthy of Waters's disputed cinematic talents.

D

LAURIEN DOMINIQUE   *aka Lailani*

Laurien Dominique moved from the Midwest to San Francisco, where she enrolled in art school. While in California, she was introduced to a very free and open social life—a striking contrast to her puritanical background. She began to experiment with some art films, and was subsequently offered adult-film roles. Her screen charm and pleasant personality soon made her quite in demand as an actress. She played many supporting roles that saved otherwise failing films.

Her most notable role was the lonely housewife in Hard Soap, Hard Soap, but she has also appeared in The Ecstasy Girls, V—The Hot One, Hot Rackets, Hot Legs, Hot and Saucy Pizza Girls, Fantasy World, The Sensuous Detective, The Budding of Brie, Screwples, and Sweet Dreams, Suzan.

Recently, she has not been active in the adult-film industry, but has not officially retired from it either.

DOWNSTAIRS/UPSTAIRS ★★

Director: Lisa Barr
Cast: Kay Parker, Seka, Sherrisse, R. J. Reynolds

This film is a fun spoof of the classic BBC series, but severely lacks the original's superb writing quality. Nevertheless, the sensual performances are very entertaining and the film is occasionally funny.

A new maid is hired into the Bun household. As she is introduced to her chores, she discovers that the family is very weird. The mother is an insatiable slut, the daughter is no better, and the father is a flasher. To spice things up, a famous pianist waltzes into the household and into the hearts and other anatomical regions of all the ladies, including the innocent new maid.

The erotic encounters are flamboyant, especially as Sherrisse and the midget cook erotically romp around the kitchen, violently dusting themselves with a sack of flour and covering their bodies with as many food stuffs as they possibly can. The scene with Kay Parker and R. J. Reynolds sensually fondling each other on the grass is wildly hilarious.

What the cast lacks in acting ability, they make up for in sheer acting indulgence, giving almost shouting-level performances. Kay Parker should be singled out for her outstanding portrayal of a highly-sexed, old woman finding love and lust with a younger man. She possesses a spark and authenticity that is refreshing in adult films.

Genre: Graphic
Year: 1980
Time: 84 min.
Acting: Good
Casting: Good

Script: Fair
Production: Good
Directing: Good
Theme: Rich Housewife, Maids
Humor: Yes

★ Watchable   ★★★ Must See
★★ Recommended   ★★★★ Masterpiece

D

DREA

Drea is a hot, energetic brunette who has just recently entered the adult-film industry. Before her career as an actress, she was a disc jockey for WDAI and WYEN—two radio stations broadcasting out of Chicago. She also spent a year getting the infamous Rich Kids, Inc. discotheque off the ground.

While in Chicago, Drea read about William Margold's exploits as an agent/sex-film star. Thinking Margold was boasting about his abilities, she came to Los Angeles and met him. It was lust and love at first sight. They are now married.

Drea's first film was Las Vegas Lady, and she has since appeared in Country Comfort, Love Goddesses, Ring of Desire, and Hot Fatigues. She will be featured in the future releases of Sinferno, Flesh Pond, and Erotikicks.

Drea is a self-proclaimed woman-hater and refuses to do any lesbian scenes, but will do anything with a man in the name of erotic art.

EASY ★★

Producer: Sam Norvell
Director: Anthony Spinelli
Cast: Jesie St. James, Jack Wright, Georgina Spelvin

This film introduced Jesie St. James in her first leading role, and is still one of her best performances to date. Jesie St. James plays a schoolteacher named Kate Harrison. She is accosted by one of the students after class and is forced into a sexual encounter with him. After a similar encounter with the student's friend, Kate quits her teaching job and moves to another city. There she tries to find love, only to end up with unsympathetic men who are only interested in uninvolved romantic quickies.

Ms. St. James is always energetic, intense, and full of love. When she has a bad experience with a man, she does not become embittered, just disappointed. She always retains hope in her search for a mate. The sex, consequently, is very realistic and full of near-convulsive action.

The film has been enormously successful critically, but because of its low-budget nature, it is often uneven technically. Compared to others in its class, however, it is better than the norm.

Genre: Graphic
Year: 1978
Time: 85 min.
Acting: Good
Casting: Good

Script: Fair
Production: Good
Directing: Very Good
Theme: Rape
Humor: No

★ Watchable   ★★★ Must See
★★ Recommended   ★★★★ Masterpiece

E

THE ECSTASY GIRLS

Producer: Harold Lime
Director: Robert McCallum
cast: Jamie Gillis, Serena, Lesllie Bovèe, Laurien Dominique, John Leslie, Paul Thomas, Georgina Spelvin

This is producer Harold Lime's best production of late, and certainly his most popular. The girls are very beautiful, the story is solid, and the erotic encounters are almost always superior.

The story is about an out-of-work young actor, played by Jamie Gillis. He is offered a job by a rich young man, who is co-heir with his four sisters to a very large estate. In an attempt to get all the money for himself, the rich brother hires the actor to photograph his sisters in sexual situations. He can then use the shots to convince their puritanical father that the girls are lewd, perverse, and unworthy of the inheritance.

The sex is hot, intense, sometimes funny and always very erotic. The scene with Laurien Dominique is soft and tender, the dungeon scene between Gillis and Serena is harsh and brutal. There is a little of everything in this film.

Technically, it is solid. The photography isn't outstanding, but it certainly isn't substandard. As a film, it is perhaps one of the most popular in recent years and one of the most exciting from an adult-entertainment point of view.

Genre: Graphic   **Script:** Very Good
Year: 1979   **Production:** Good
Time: 97 min.   **Directing:** Very Good
Acting: Good   **Theme:** Rich Girls
Casting: Good   **Humor:** Yes

EDUCATION OF THE BARONESS ★★★

Director: Sudha Nud
Cast: Brigitte La Haye, Susan Deloir, Aude LeCoeur,
Robert Lourge Albar

One adult-film historian, named this the best foreign sex film of the year 1980. It certainly merits the praise. While the story is typical of French erotic comedies, it is done with such good taste and humor that it is a lot of fun to watch.

The film is about a very aristocratic couple who are into masochism. In pursuing their exotic tastes, they decide to switch places with their servants. The maid becomes the baroness, and the chauffeur becomes the baron. This proves to be a bonanza for the two servants, who now have a chance to taste what power and wealth is all about. The real baron and baroness are ecstatic because they can taste what it is like to be on the wrong end of the social strata.

In the course of the film, we are taken through a number of very swift sexual episodes, full of beautiful hitchhikers, exotic love affairs, gourmet sex, some whips and chains, and a little light S&M—but all in good taste. The movie doesn't set out to shock, or to cater to fans of brutal sex. It lets the audience be teased by playful dominance and submission. There's no other way to describe it except to say that it is very *French*.

Genre: Graphic
Year: 1980
Time: 112 min.
Acting: Good
Casting: Good

Script: Good
Production: Very Good
Directing: Good
Theme: Maid
Humor: Yes

★ Watchable	★★★ Must See
★★ Recommended	★★★★ Masterpiece

E

ERIC EDWARDS

Eric Edwards has worked continually in the adult-film industry for almost ten years. He was involved in the early adult classic, The Private Afternoons of Pamela Mann, directed by Henry Paris. He has amassed a credit list that rivals John Holmes and Jamie Gillis (the only other male actor who has constantly worked for ten years), but has unfortunately not received as much acclaim. He is a better actor than Holmes and can match most of what Jamie Gillis has done. His more memorable films include Debbie Does Dallas, Pussycat Ranch, Babylon Pink, The Budding of Brie, Platinum Paradise, Misbehavin', The Taking of Christina, American Pie, Blonde Ambition, Dirty Lilly, Neon Nights, Slip-Up, The Affairs of Janice, Sweet Cakes, Urban Cowgirls, and The Opening of Misty Beethoven. He is starring in the soon-to-be-released Damon Christian film Titillation, where he plays a Phillip Marlowe type of down-and-out detective.

He has strong features and has confidently played roles ranging from street punks to middle-aged businessmen.

800 FANTASY LANE ★★

Producer/director: Svetlana
Photo: Robert McCallum
Cast: Jamie Gillis, Chris Anderson, Amy Leigh, Bud Wise

This film is a valiant first-time effort by a very pretty female director, Svetlana. It is uneven, but contains some very creative episodes that would place it among the best all-time adult films.

The story is about two gas-station attendants who are fed up with their boring job. On a lark, they decide to pose as two oil-rich tycoons looking for a house in Los Angeles. They call an all-female realty company, and plan to enjoy as much sex as they can with the girls before being found out. The girls, thinking the guys are really loaded, cater to their erotic fantasies, but the plot suddenly diverts into some very bizarre sequences.

These exotic adventures take one of the boys into a tub filled with five gorgeous, naked ladies; into a dungeon with girls strapped in leather trapezes; and into a cage filled with man-eating tiger-ladies.

The technical quality often dips below standard, but some scenes are beautifully photographed, nonetheless. The film's strong point is in its uninhibited, raw creativity.

Genre: Graphic   **Script:** Fair
Year: 1979   **Production:** Good
Time: 82 min.   **Directing:** Good
Acting: Fair   **Theme:** Sales Girls
Casting: Good   **Humor:** No

★ Watchable   ★★★ Must See
★★ Recommended   ★★★★ Masterpiece

E

8 TO 4

Director: Louis Lewis
Cast: Annette Haven, Loni Sanders, Veronica Hart,
Lisa DeLeeuw

If this film is trying to be a spoof of 9 to 5 with Dolly Parton, it doesn't succeed.

Annette Haven, Loni Sanders, and Lisa DeLeeuw play three underpaid, overworked secretaries for a very sexist boss. The girls, however, seem to really love the sexual abuse, and it is a little weird when they turn on the boss.

While the sex scenes are varied and energetic, they run too long and deaden rather than support the story line. We are given, however, an abundance of erotic antics, which should be quite amusing for adult film fans. Both Loni Sanders and Veronica Hart are adorable, but Lisa DeLeeuw's foul-mouthed, aggressive persona doesn't command much sympathy from her audience.

Director Louis Lewis has made an art out of adapting Hollywood themes for adult audiences. His only saving grace is in putting a lot of pretty bodies on screen.

Genre: Graphic
Year: 1981
Time: 75 min.
Acting: Fair
Casting: Fair

Script: Poor
Production: Good
Directing: Fair
Theme: Secretaries
Humor: Yes

"11"

Director: Louis Lewis
Cast: Brooke West, Dhaije Taan, Jon Martin

This pretentious spoof of Blake Edwards' 10 is long on sex and short on humor.

Jon Martin plays a man suffering from impotence who goes to a sex clinic for some help. Suddenly, he sees a woman that fits his fantasy image of the "perfect" female—trim body, big breasts, succulent mouth, full lips, and so forth. Off he goes on a crazed odyssey searching for this phantom woman. Meanwhile, he continues the sex therapy which helps him romantically, but drains his pocketbook.

The plot affords a lot of room for sensual exploitation, which often ends up in long, tedious, graphic displays of interlocking humans. What jokes there are tend to be forced and uninspired.

Genre: Graphic	**Script:** Poor
Year: 1980	**Production:** Good
Time: 90 min.	**Directing:** Fair
Acting: Fair	**Theme:** Sex Therapy
Casting: Good	**Humor:** Yes

★ Watchable	★★★ Must See
★★ Recommended	★★★★ Masterpiece

E

EL TOPO ★★★

Director: Alexandro Jodorowsky
Cast: Alexandro Jodorowsky, Mara Lorenzio,
   Brontis Jodorowsky

This was one of the first midnight-movie cult hits because of its visually stunning, mentally exciting indulgence in sex and violence.

El Topo rides into a town whose population has just been massacred. He shoots some of the men responsible and castrates their leader. He leaves his seven-year-old son with some monks and departs with the gang leader's woman, Mara. In the desert, he brutalizes her, then quasi-rapes her, and she quickly falls in love with him. After their frantic love-making, she tells him that he can prove that he's the best by killing the four masters. For no apparent reason other than to please Mara, El Topo begins his quest, outwitting and killing each of the four masters. When he's finished, El Topo feels so guilty about what he's done that he allows himself to be shot up by Mara and a mysterious woman in black. The two women then make love while El Topo lies bleeding and dying.

The film has been quite controversial, some critics labeling it degenerate, others claiming that it is a confusing mess of self-indulgence by its Chilean-born director. While there is some truth to both claims, the film has a raw, creative drive that makes it quite compelling. It is not for the weak of heart.

El Topo rapidly developed a very strong and loyal audience during its initial release and it would probably have done much better with better distribution over the last decade.

Genre: Taboo   **Script:** Very Good
Year: 1971   **Production:** Good
Time: 123 min.   **Directing:** Excellent
Acting: Very Good   **Theme:** Rape
Casting: Good   **Humor:** No

EMMANUELLE ★★

Producer: Yves Rousset Rouard
Director: Just Jaeckin
Cast: Sylvia Kristel, Alain Cuny, Marika Green

Emmanuelle is a soft, seductive film that has been enormously popular in America despite some very bad reviews. It is also one of the first sex-oriented films to have attempted a general distribution. In fact, it was Columbia Pictures that released it in America. It is an elegant, excellently photographed movie, but too often wallows in a syrupy pretention.

It is about a young, French woman who joins her husband in Thailand. There, she is taunted by many of her fellow society ladies for being too prudish and reserved, and for not ever having had an affair. She eventually does have an affair— many of them—with both men and women. But it isn't until she seeks the help of a lover/instructor named Mario and is raped in a smoke-filled opium den, that she begins to understand what bestial lust is all about. Having sampled it, she realizes that she wants it, and goes for more.

There are a number of soft, lesbian encounters very typical of French cinema, coupled with encounters with handsome, sensitive men who enjoy superficial lovemaking. Some of the scenes are tender, others warmly brutal. The film never really deals with sex in a realistic manner, just a bombardment of soft, well-photographed, sensual images and an over-blown, continuous repeating of its erotic philosophy.

Genre: Erotic
Year: 1974
Time: 92 min.
Acting: Good
Casting: Good

Script: Fair
Production: Very Good
Directing: Fair
Theme: Lesbian
Humor: No

★ Watchable ★★★ Must See
★★ Recommended ★★★★ Masterpiece

E

EMMANUELLE, THE JOYS OF A WOMAN ★★

Director: Francis Giacobetti
Cast: Sylvia Kristel, Umberto Orsini, Catherine Rivet

This is the follow up film to *Emmanuelle*. Like the first one, *Joys of a Woman* wallows in pseudo-philosophy while displaying a lot of aroused women seeking fulfillment.

The setting is Hong Kong, where Emmanuelle is taken through the high-life of the aristocrat. In the first film, Emmanuelle was sexually reserved, and came out as she discovered her hidden sensuality. In the sequel, she explores further into the erotic realm—especially other women—in trying to find the perfect lover.

The characters are not real, but ethereal, dream-like creatures floating through life. This quality actually works quite well as Sylvia Kristel encounters other women. The eroticism is soft and sensual. When she confronts a man, however, there is a feeling only of performance. It's much more brisk or rushed. The male lovers never seem to be as compassionate or as feeling as the women, nor are their characters as developed.

The photography is quite lush, and has captured a postcard view of modern Hong Kong. The movie is very chic, and some of the erotic encounters are very nice, but the film has no heart. Because of this, it may become tedious for some.

Genre: Erotic
Year: 1976
Time: 100 min.
Acting: Good
Casting: Good

Script: Fair
Production: Very Good
Directing: Fair
Theme: Lesbian
Humor: No

THE EROTIC ADVENTURES OF CANDY ★★

Producer/director: Gail Palmer
Cast: Carol Connors, John Holmes, Georgina Spelvin, Turk
Lyon, Paul Thomas

This was Carol Connors' first truly fun film. It is a delightful,
colorful picture with a lot of variation in the sexual encounters. Sometimes it becomes a little too tedious in its pretentious sexual philosophy. But on the whole, it is a very well-
made film.

The story begins with Candy at home, where she has her
first sexual experience with the gardener. Being adventurous
and curious, she decides to go off into the world to see what's
there. She lands in some very strange and erotic situations.
She is picked up by a jogging John Holmes who complains to
her about his "deformity." She visits a gynecologist who takes
advantage of the situation, and finally ends up in a love cult
that practices the art of making love around the clock.

The sex is funny, innocent, playful, and indulgently
explicit. But once we get into the cult, and its wide open orgy
scene, the film gets a little too preachy.

Carol Connors is rapturous in her innocence and charm,
and this film is without a doubt her most appealing performance in an adult film.

Genre: Graphic
Year: 1978
Time: 85 min.
Acting: Fair
Casting: Good

Script: Fair
Production: Very Good
Directing: Good
Theme: Young Girl
Humor: Yes

★ Watchable ★★★ Must See
★★ Recommended ★★★★ Masterpiece

E

ERUPTION ★★½

Director: Stanley Kurlan
Cast: John Holmes, Lesllie Bovée, Susan Hart

The tropics are noted mainly for two things: great scenery and steamy, uninhibited sex. This film has got them both.

John Holmes plays an insurance salesman. The wife of a super-rich man sets up a policy for one million dollars then plans to rub him out with the help of John Holmes. The problem is the lady's daughter, who is just as devious as her mother. The daughter cuts her mother out of the action and joins up with the crooked insurance man.

The sex is hot, sweaty, and varied. Of note, there is a very good scene where the perky daughter, a girlfriend, and a muscle man explore each other in a gym. Lesllie Bovée, of course, is always able to blend chic personality with hard sex.

Shot on location in Hawaii, the photography is quite nice, capturing some of the lush environment in vibrant and rich colors. It compliments the eroticism. The story, however, sometimes bogs down, but the main thrust is to create a setting for an erotic play. In that regard, the film succeeds quite well.

Genre: Graphic	**Script:** Good
Year: 1978	**Production:** Very Good
Time: 85 min.	**Directing:** Good
Acting: Good	**Theme:** Tropical Women
Casting: Very Good	**Humor:** Some

EVERYTHING YOU ALWAYS WANTED TO KNOW ABOUT SEX BUT WERE AFRAID TO ASK ★★½

Director: Woody Allen
Cast: Woody Allen, Gene Wilder, Tony Randall

This is a very funny spoof of pop sex-psychology literature. The film is included here because it is entirely about sexual perversions, even though it is not technically erotic.

Allen has taken some of the most popular clinical treatments of sexual fetishes and has placed them into very strange situations. Gene Wilder, for example, falls in love with a sheep. Woody Allen plays a medieval court jester who gets his lance stuck in his lady's chastity belt while the king is off fighting in the Crusades. A giant breast is unleashed onto the countryside. An Italian couple can only find happiness in public sex. And we are taken into the inner workings of a male human body as it attempts to seduce a woman in a car.

Each individual scene is quite well done. The tales are swift, punchy, and filled with satire about the overly exaggerated importance of sex in our culture.

Genre: Erotic	**Script:** Very Good
Year: 1972	**Production:** Good
Time: 88 min.	**Directing:** Good
Acting: Good	**Theme:** Sex Perversions
Casting: Very Good	**Humor:** Yes

★	Watchable	★★★	Must See
★★	Recommended	★★★★	Masterpiece

E

EXHAUSTED ★★★

Producer/director: Julia St. Vincent
Cast: John Holmes, Seka, Bob Chinn

This film is an attempt at a bona fide documentary of famous sex star John Holmes. It's a different venture for adult filmmakers, and one that really pays off. It's enlightening, informative, and quite attractive.

The film begins as passing pedestrians are asked if they have ever heard of John Holmes. The responses are varied and quite funny. But unlike many of the fake documentaries in the adult industry, this one does not attempt to recreate the performer's lusty life, but sits down to discuss it with him. Also interviewed are Seka and one of Holmes' directors, who describe what it was like to work with him. Holmes also tells us about himself, his career, and his attitude toward women.

The movie is not without its erotic moments. We are often shown clips from many of his better films. These clips come in groups, and are usually thematic. Where he talks about oral sex, for example, we see examples from many of his films.

The editing is very neatly done, swift, and never tedious. Many of the interviews are short and to the point. This documentary succeeds where most others fail: It offers true insight into a film star's personality.

Genre: Graphic
Year: 1981
Time: 80 min.
Acting: Good
Casting: Good

Script: Good
Production: Good
Directing: Very Good
Theme: John Holmes
Humor: Yes

EXPOSED ★★★

Director: Jeffrey Fairbanks
Cast: John Leslie, Shirley Woods, Georgina Spelvin, Kitty Shayne, John Martin, Lysa Thatcher

A very strong story and a great directorial debut by young Jeffrey Fairbanks make this a top-notch adult film.

Willie Gordon, a porn star who quit the business, gets married and settles down with a sweet, suburban wife. A next-door neighbor finds out about Gordon's past and blackmails him into making love with her. Word gets back to a sleazy producer who pays Gordon a visit, and once again he is being blackmailed, this time into doing one last sex film. Willie reluctantly agrees.

The sex scenes grow nicely out of the plot, between the husband and wife, between Gordon and the neighbor, and finally back on the set of an erotic film shoot.

The film reflects the care and planning of its fledgling director. While it's not a blockbuster, the performances are solid and well worth a look.

Genre: Graphic
Year: 1980
Time: 86 min.
Acting: Good
Casting: Very Good

Script: Very Good
Production: Good
Directing: Very Good
Theme: Sex Film Star
Humor: Yes

★ Watchable ★★★ Must See
★★ Recommended ★★★★ Masterpiece

E

EXPOSE ME LOVELY ★★★

Producer/Director: Armond Weston
Cast: Jennifer Welles, Ras Kean, Cary Lacy (Catherine
    Burgess), Jody Maxwell

Many adult films often try copying other films, then spicing
them up with a lot of sex. This erotic detective film seems to
break the pattern. Its original story, good performances, and
great erotic scenes rate it three stars.

A pretty lady shows up at Frosty's detective agency and
hires him to find her missing brother. Frosty takes on the job
and enters a labyrinth of misinformation, kooky ladies, wrong
turns, false leads, and utter confusion. The plot becomes so
twisted that narration is needed to keep it straight.

A scene with an exotic artist (Jody Maxwell) is wild and
intensely erotic, as is his coincidental meeting with his ex-
wife, which also turns into an empassioned embrace.

The film has been very popular on late-night cable stations,
but many of its more graphic sex scenes have been cut. This
actually helps the film move even faster through its convoluted plot.

Genre: Graphic
Year: 1976
Time: 90 min.
Acting: Good
Casting: Good

Script: Very Good
Production: Good
Directing: Good
Theme: Detective
Humor: Yes

Director: Svetlana
Cast: Annette Haven, John Leslie, Chris Anderson, Rhonda Jo Petty, Kandi Barbour, Seka

This very ambitious film tries to mix reality and fantasy and doesn't quite succeed. Still, its offbeat style, strange adventures, and very exotic girls make it well worth seeing.

A man with a flat tire stops at a house to use the phone. It is no ordinary house—in fact, it has some very weird features, including life-sized dolls that suddenly turn into sex-crazed women, and a kind of giant vagina that swallows men whole.

All the sets are quite imaginative and the sex extremely graphic, but it often goes on too long. Despite its creative bursts, many of the sets are too cramped, too small, and the camera is often out of touch with what the actors are doing. It tries too hard to be creative, and if the filmmakers had just relaxed a bit, the film might have been much more fun.

Genre: Graphic
Year: 1980
Time: 90 min.
Acting: Fair
Casting: Fair

Script: Fair
Production: Good
Directing: Fair
Theme: Sex Experiments
Humor: Yes

★ Watchable   ★★★ Must See
★★ Recommended   ★★★★ Masterpiece

F

FANTASY

Director: Gerard Damiano
Cast: Georgina Spelvin, Kyoto Sun, Jon Martin, Brooke West, Lisa Moreau

This spoof of television's *Fantasy Island* focuses exclusively on erotic fantasies. There's no story, just nonstop sex.

A young bride, for example, daydreams about offbeat and bizarre sexual acts and whether or not her husband would be shocked if she suggested that they indulged in same. Another young couple is so jaded that they can't get excited unless it's with a group, and so on.

The sex is constant and varied, and caters to just about every sensual lust imaginable, in glowing graphic detail. Many fans of adult cinema have rated this film extremely high for its intense eroticism. It has become very popular, largely due to the performances of Georgina Spelvin, Kyoto Sun, and the very sensual Brooke West.

Genre: Graphic
Year: 1979
Time: 90 min.
Acting: Fair
Casting: Fair

Script: Fair
Production: Good
Directing: Good
Theme: Swinging Couples
Humor: Yes

FANTASY WORLD ★★

Directors: Bob Chinn and Jeffrey Fairbanks
Cast: Jesie St. James, Laurien Dominique, Sharon Kane, James
   Price, John Martin

Fantasy World is an excellent example of the sex-fantasy
genre. A lot of the cinematography is exotic and colorful,
some of the sequences are delightfully offbeat and fun.

   Three sailors visit a fantasy club in San Francisco. As the
cabaret-type show begins, each sailor starts to feel something
strange happening to him. Suddenly, each is living out an
unbelievably "real" erotic dream.

   This sort of framing provides the film with a good excuse to
jump from one highly erotic encounter to another without
having to tie them together. One sailor finds himself on a
desert isle with a couple of stunning girls. Another finds himself seducing a female piano player. But the film's highlight is
the all-out orgiastic party at the end.

   This is a creative film that lets the exotic dreams flow at
their own speed. It never pushes or forces the creative ele-
ment, and never gets dull. As an adult film it is done in surprisingly good taste.

Genre: Graphic   **Script:** Good
Year: 1979   **Production:** Good
Time: 78 min.   **Directing:** Fair
Acting: Fair   **Theme:** Dream Girls
Casting: Good   **Humor:** Yes

★ Watchable	★★★ Must See
★★ Recommended	★★★★ Masterpiece

F

FASCINATION ★★★

Director: Larry Revene
Cast: Ron Jeremy, Candida Royalle, Samantha Fox,
Merle Michaels

This is the Walter Mitty story in an adult film. It's fun, raw, sympathetic, and often uneven, but vastly entertaining and erotic. It ranks very high for these reasons.

Ernie Gordon is a born loser, a total washout with women. He buys a book on how to seduce women and follows the instructions step by step, but something always goes wrong. He gets a gorgeous blonde in bed, but her husband comes home early. He hires a hooker only to find out that she is a he.

The sexual encounters are mixed with eros and pathos; some are teasing, some quite explicit, but always humorous. The film's strong point is in the actor playing Ernie (Ron Jeremy). He's a short, dark, plump performer who actually does a remarkable job. He is so adorably bad that both men and women will sympathize with his problems. As an adult film, this one's unique.

Genre: Graphic
Year: 1980
Time: 79 min.
Acting: Good
Casting: Very Good

Script: Good
Production: Good
Directing: Good
Theme: Loser
Humor: Yes

FELICIA ★★

Director: Max Pecas
Cast: Rebecca Brooke, Beatrice Hart, Ann Roche

This is a French film that takes itself too seriously. As a result, it is neither serious nor humorous enough to really hit the mark.

Felicia is a young schoolgirl. Her mother has gone to Australia and left her with a couple for the summer vacation. Felicia is not happy with the arrangement, but is intrigued with the couple's lovemaking habits. She repeatedly sneaks down the hall late at night to listen. Finally, she is drawn toward the husband and has an affair. The wife finds out and has an affair with Felicia, spinning the plot further into its sensual complications.

The erotic encounters build logically from the basic premise. Felicia spends a lot of time getting acquainted with the couple and experimenting with her own sensuality. That, strangely, is the film's major failing. It is too lethargic, too serious about her coming of age to support such a careful study. Both *Therese and Isabelle* and *Bilitis* have covered the same ground, but with much finer craftsmanship.

Genre: Graphic
Year: 1977
Time: 98 min.
Acting: Fair
Casting: Fair

Script: Fair
Production: Good
Directing: Fair
Theme: Schoolgirls
Humor: Yes

★ Watchable   ★★★ Must See
★★ Recommended   ★★★★ Masterpiece

F

FEMALE TROUBLE

Director: John Waters
Cast: Divine, David Lochary, Mink Stole, Edith Massey

Many have claimed that *Female Trouble* is John Waters's best film. Maybe so. *Female Trouble* is certainly his least offensive.

The story is about Divine—the all-American female beauty. Of course, the grotesque and fat female impersonater could hardly be termed either a "beauty" or a "female," but this is the film's premise. She runs away from her mean parents and ends up being raped by a passing motorist. Years later, after a career in crime, she is drawn into the confidence of the owners of a beauty salon who are doing a pictorial study of crime. They believe that the more criminal one becomes, the more beautiful one gets. They tell Divine that she is one of the most beautiful persons they've ever seen, and want her to model for them. The vain Divine jumps at the chance for exhibition.

Waters's displays of social taboos are meant to shock and repel his audience, but he does it with such zest and wit that most viewers chuckle rather than become nauseous, although the latter is a possibility for those who are accustomed to a more traditional style of filmmaking. Such displays include gore, disfigurement, open sexuality, fetishes, torture, and vomit.

Waters's biggest success is with the people he casts. Edith Massey, Divine, Vivian Pearce are so unusual and yet so full of life that they do have a strange sort of screen presence. These people know who they are, both relishing the exhibitionism and snubbing society for its intolerance.

Genre: Taboo	**Script:** Fair
Year: 1974	**Production:** Poor
Time: 95 min.	**Directing:** Very Good
Acting: Fair	**Theme:** Beauty Salon, Models
Casting: Excellent	**Humor:** Yes

F

FIONA ON FIRE

Producer/director: Kenneth Schwartz (Warren Evans)
Cast: Amber Hunt, Sam Dean, Jamie Gillis, Gloria Leonard,
  Marlene Willoughby

Another superior adult detective film, this one having a good
story and lusty sexual encounters.

The film begins with the brutal, shotgun murder of a
woman, Via Fiona. A black cop is put on the case and he
begins searching among the woman's possessions for a lead.
He find her diary, reads it, and we flash back to a number of
steamy, indulgent romantic affairs in the woman's past.

Production values are quite high and the treatment of the
sex is top-notch. While Amber Hunt has a few acting problems, her erotic scenes remain consistently steamy and fun.
Marlene Willoughby and Jamie Gillis give outstanding performances as an incestuous mother and son.

Fiona on Fire combines excellent cinematography with excellent, graphic sex. Very few adult films attempt this, let
alone bring it off.

Genre: Graphic	**Script:** Very Good
Year: 1978	**Production:** Very Good
Time: 113 min.	**Directing:** Good
Acting: Good	**Theme:** Detective
Casting: Very Good	**Humor:** Yes

★	Watchable	★★★	Must See
★★	Recommended	★★★★	Masterpiece

F

FLESH GORDON ★

Director: Michael Benveniste, Howard Ziehm
Cast: Jason Williams, Suzanne Fields, Joseph Hudgins

The problem with spoofing old television serials such as Flash Gordon and Buck Rogers is that they are already spoofs of themselves. *Flesh Gordon* is not very well made, the acting ranges from bad to real bad, and the writing is lame. But for some reason, it has charm.

A sex ray is ravishing the earth, producing uncontrollable orgies across the globe. Flesh Gordon and Dr. Jerkoff blast off to find the source of this wicked device and end up on the Planet Porno, battling wicked Amazons, lusty lesbians, perverts, and monsters.

Much of the original sex scenes have been clipped from the current editions of the film, which is perhaps for the better. The film already suffers from idiotic situations and to prolong them would only make it worse. But it is because of its silliness and ineptitude that the film is so charming. It is filled with exotic sexual encounters, some visually sensual girls, and countless puns on sex and erotic filmmaking.

The special effects — stop-motion animation! — during the ending sequence where the hero battles a giant is quite well done for a low-budget film. In fact, many of the effects are a big improvement over the original series.

Genre: Erotic	**Script:** Good
Year: 1974	**Production:** Poor
Time: 90 min.	**Directing:** Good
Acting: Poor	**Theme:** Science Fiction, Space Girls
Casting: Good	**Humor:** Yes

FOR RICHER, FOR POORER ★½

Producer/director: Gerard Damiano
Cast: Georgina Spelvin, Richard Bolla, Bobby Astyr, Mary Margaret, Debbie Revenge

This film was Damiano's attempt at a serious movie, but it didn't quite come off. It deserves a star for being as well made as the bulk of adult films and another half star for its brave attempt at something different.

The story is about loneliness and divorce. We are told about a failing marriage through a series of flashbacks. We see the young, sexually electric couple newly married, then the eventual decline of mutual attraction. They look elsewhere for romance and finally the woman is alone and desperate.

Georgina Spelvin plays the divorced woman with her usual high-strung acting ability and intensely erotic bedside manner. The film contains some very powerful sex scenes, due to Spelvin's ability, but not as much as one would expect for a Damiano epic.

The story, while a valiant effort, often sinks into sappy sayings and superficial generalities. Damiano's talent lies in his humor and offbeat approach to sex, not in being dramatic.

Genre: Graphic	**Script:** Fair
Year: 1980	**Production:** Good
Time: 90 min.	**Directing:** Fair
Acting: Very Good	**Theme:** Divorce
Casting: Good	**Humor:** No

★	Watchable	★★★	Must See
★★	Recommended	★★★★	Masterpiece

F

FOR THE LOVE OF PLEASURE ★★

Director: Edwin S. Brown
Cast: Annette Haven, Jamie Gillis, Samantha Fox, Kyoto, Veri Knotty

An erotic heaven-and-hell spoof that contains some very funny ideas about both places. It is playful and very erotic.

A burglar caught plying his trade tries to flee and is shot and killed. For some reason, he goes to heaven and finds that the world's concept of the holy realm is incredibly wrong.

He finds sexy angels, great food, and a plethora of erotic pleasures. The film doesn't take a back seat or a shy approach to the burglar's indulgences, but shows us everything he partakes of. The only problem is that it becomes too much of a good thing.

The photography is above average and the delightful story is a solid example of superior adult programming.

Genre: Graphic
Year: 1980
Time: 71 min.
Acting: Fair
Casting: Good

Script: Good
Production: Good
Directing: Good
Theme: Angels
Humor: Yes

★ Watchable ★★★ Must See
★★ Recommended ★★★★ Masterpiece

SAMANTHA FOX

Samantha Fox was born and raised in New York City. As a girl she studied ballet and modern dance. By the end of her high school years, she was dancing professionally. Before getting into adult films, she was a co-host for a local cable television show. Chuck Vincent cast her in 1978 for the leading role in Bad Penny, where she gained some repute as an actress. Samantha went on to star in numerous films, winning the Erotica Award two years in a row for Jack 'n Jill (1980) and This Lady is a Tramp (1981).

Samantha has a strong presence on screen. She is able to bring out some taut characterizations ranging from a young, innocent girl to a tough, mean, foul-mouthed woman.

Her most memorable films are: The Tiffany Minx, Mystique, October Silk, Her Name Was Lisa, Amanda by Night, Pink Ladies, Foxtrot, Roommates, and Outlaw Ladies.

F

FOXTROT

Producer/director: Cecil Howard
Cast: Marlene Willoughby, Veronica Hart, Samantha Fox,
  Sharon Mitchell, Richard Bolla, David Morris

This is a new film that has already received a lot of favorable
notices for its eroticism and its attempt to seriously probe its
characters' sex lives.

The story takes place during a New Year's party and we
move into the lives of each of the guests. We see a stripper
with delusions of being an actress, the affair between a bored
housewife and an erotic writer, and a famous movie director
sexually manipulating his underlings. The party moves
toward its climax as the people get drunk, boisterous, and
aroused.

The sex is swift, but still caters to fans of adult films. The
advantage here is that the picture does such a good job of
presenting its characters, we are drawn into their lives and
begin to share their lusts, their desires, their happinesses and
their defeats.

For what it sets out to do, *Foxtrot* does a very nice job. Cecil
Howard has always been noted for superior production values
and for his ability to bring out both honest and erotic performances from his cast. This film will undoubtedly continue
to grow in popularity and prestige.

Genre: Graphic
Year: 1982
Time: 90 min.
Acting: Very Good
Casting: Good

Script: Good
Production: Very Good
Directing: Very Good
Theme: Party Girls
Humor: Yes

FRITZ THE CAT ★★

Director: Ralph Bakshi

This was one of the first feature-length adult cartoons. Its debut was considered raunchy, shocking, and very entertaining.

The story concerns a classic 60's hero, Fritz, and his adventures through the urban underground. He loves sex and constantly professes the glories of revolution. At first he is content with just sex, but as the story moves through exotic adventures he discovers that the only way he can truly be a revolutionary is to join up with one of the militant groups. There, he's over his head.

In sharp contrast to Walt Disney's fluffy characters, Fritz is seen servicing a bunch of screaming female cats, popping drugs, and having loads of fun. We are taken through Harlem where, in this case, the blacks are portrayed as jive-talking crows. *Fritz* is not a fantasy, but an animation venture into super-reality, at least as Bakshi sees it.

The animation is crude, but very effective. It has a raw, gutsy energy that brings out some of the social issues of the tumultuous sixties.

Genre: Erotic
Year: 1972
Time: 78 min.
Animation: Good

Script: Good
Directing: Good
Theme: Urban Underground
Humor: Yes

★ Watchable   ★★★ Must See
★★ Recommended   ★★★★ Masterpiece

G

GAMES WOMEN PLAY

Producer/director: Chuck Vincent
Cast: Lesllie Bovèe, Samantha Fox, Roger Caine, Jack
  Wrangler, Merle Michaels

A sophisticated adult comedy with surprising verve and
polish. The performances are spunky and the technical aspects worthy of note.

The film is about five glamour models living in the fast-
paced world of New York's mega-dollar advertising industry.
The girls are often given to playing erotic games with their
boyfriends and husbands, and with each other. The action is
episodic, but the story folds back on itself, ending in one of
the most sensual games of poker ever filmed.

The frequent sex is in good taste, more so than in most
Chuck Vincent movies. The erotic scenes always rise out of
the girls playing with the guys. One teases a man in the stair-
way of a Manhattan office building, and it turns into a bold
erotic embrace. The highlight is the multi-couple bash as the
married couples exchange partners.

Despite the emphasis on the erotic sequences, the film retains a strong story line with enough room for the characters
to develop. Chuck Vincent has a gift for wringing excellent
performances from his cast, and this film is no exception.

Genre: Graphic	**Script:** Good
Year: 1980	**Production:** Very Good
Time: 87 min.	**Directing:** Very Good
Acting: Good	**Theme:** Models
Casting: Very Good	**Humor:** Yes

JAMIE GILLIS

This dark haired muscular actor claims to be the top stud in the adult film business. Jamie Gillis has amassed quite a long list of credits and some repute as an actor. He is known for his sadistic and domineering tendencies. He won the Erotica Award for best acting three times: The Opening of Misty Beethoven (1977), A Coming of Angels (1978), and The Ecstasy Girls (1980). Jamie Gillis is one of the few actors who can blend dynamic acting with some intensely provocative sex.

Since an early age, Jamie has been interested in acting. While he performed in a number of plays in New York, he worked part time as a cab driver. He decided to change to a less demanding job, and answered an ad for nude modeling. The ad led him to the set of an adult film.

His acting background quickly became apparent, and he was soon cast in a number of leading roles. Some of his more popular films include Amanda by Night, 800 Fantasy Lane, The Private Afternoons of Pamela Mann, The Story of Joanna, Through the Looking-Glass, Taxi Girls, Coed Fever, Screwples, Roommates, Serena, Neon Nights, Pandora's Mirror and Anna Obsessed.

G

A GIRL'S BEST FRIEND

Director: Henri Pachard
Cast: Juliet Anderson, Ron Jeremy, Veronica Hart,
  Bobby Astyr

A tongue-in-cheek sex comedy, well done and well plotted.
The comedy goes for light chuckles more than belly laughs.
The performances are not heavy or dramatic, nor is the eroti-
cism even intense, but all of it is delightful, nonetheless.

An adorable mother-and-son jewel-thief team, in the tradi-
tion of Robin Hood, steal only from the ridiculously rich.
They are looking for a famous diamond and have to attend a
decadent party to which only the most elite have been invited.

The mother and son are almost discovered by their former
victims, and have to resort to heavy lovemaking to mask their
true identity. Other erotic sequences grow similarly out of the
plot, humorously and sensuously, but the director never lingers on them. The plot and the eroticism build to a stunning
climax.

Genre: Graphic
Year: 1981
Time: 84 min.
Acting: Good
Casting: Good

Script: Good
Production: Very Good
Directing: Very Good
Theme: Incest
Humor: Yes

HARD SOAP, HARD SOAP ★★½

Director: Bob Chinn
Cast: Laurien Dominique, Candida Royalle, John Holmes

A very appealing film due to its low-key humor and care-free sex.

Laurien Dominique plays the mentally disintegrating wife of a psychoanalyst who's impotent. The milkman takes too long during their morning sex affair. Her best girlfriend is sexually fulfilled, and she isn't. To put back the spark in their marriage, she decides to help her husband at the office, and ends up in a group session that turns into an orgy.

The erotic scenes are typically adult formats, but so laid-back that they're funny. Laurien nonchalantly asks the milk-man, who is in the throes of erotic rapture, how long he's going to take because she's got a friend coming over soon.

The humor is so understated that the laughs have a kind of built-in delay.

Genre: Graphic
Year: 1977
Time: 78 min.
Acting: Good
Casting: Very Good

Script: Good
Production: Fair
Directing: Good
Theme: Housewife
Humor: Yes

★ Watchable   ★★★ Must See
★★ Recommended   ★★★★ Masterpiece

H

Ms. Hart was born in Las Vegas where she graduated from high school at the age of 16. She received a B.A. from the University of Nevada in Theatrical Arts. After three years in England, where she modeled and danced professionally, she moved to New York City. She continued working as a model, trying to get into the film industry. A tenant in her apartment building suggested that she look into doing adult films. And the rest is history.

She made her adult film debut in 1980, with a bit part in the movie Fascination. Her charisma was instantly recognized and she quickly received a number of offers. She has starred in a wide variety of films, including Scent of Heather, Amanda by Night, Pandora's Mirror, Delicious, Neon Nights, Roommates, Centerspread Girls, Foxtrot, and Outlaw Ladies.

Veronica Hart has recently married. In private life, she is a sweet homebody who has the same goals and desires as most middle-class American women.

ANNETTE HAVEN

Most people agree that Annette Haven is the most beautiful actress in adult films. Annette enjoys her work and has enthusiastically embraced the adult-film industry. She has actually turned down some more prestigious R-rated horror-film projects because of their excessive violence, which she believes can be very psychologically damaging. In contrast, she thinks that sex portrayed in a sensitive, loving way is both helpful and necessary in today's society.

Ms. Haven was introduced to the adult-film world by Bonnie Holliday. Bonnie had appeared in a few of Alex DeRenzy's films, and suggested that Annette meet him for a possible role in one of his films. DeRenzy immediately cast her in his next film. She has since appeared in quite a few of the better-made adult films, including Barbara Broadcast, A Coming of Angels, Sex World, Autobiography of a Flea, Anna Obsessed, V—The Hot One, Take Off, Wicked Sensations, and A Thousand and One Erotic Nights.

She won the 1978 Erotica Award for Best Supporting Actress in the film A Coming of Angels.

H

THE HEALTH SPA ★

Director: Clair Dia
Cast: Abigail Clayton, Kay Parker, Phaery I. Burd,
John Seeman

This is a therapeutic film. Both the film and its story are single-minded about one thing—the glories of sex—and there's a reluctant attraction to its rather blatant and uninhibited approach.

An investigative reporter (Kay Parker) is sent to a health spa to unmask what may be a deception to the public. The spa claims to have found a weight-reduction plan that uses sexual activity as a catalyst. The reporter goes, but is soon drawn into a lesbian encounter with a very attractive young lady (Abigail Clayton), and is converted, not to its weight-reduction plan, but to its unique method of exercise.

The film contains so many erotic sequences that the story line is often an intrusion. This may be good or bad, depending on what you desire in an adult film. But on the whole, this is a tedious film, spiced only by an occasional creative scene. The treatment of the lesbian encounters, however, is worthy of attention. The film was directed by a former erotic performer, Clair Dia.

Genre: Graphic
Year: 1978
Time: 81 min.
Acting: Fair
Casting: Good

Script: Fair
Production: Good
Directing: Fair
Theme: Athletic Girls
Humor: No

HER NAME WAS LISA ★

Director: Richard Mahler
Cast: Samantha Fox, Vanessa Del Rio, Jake Stuart

This is a very moody film that tries to seriously study the sexual nature of a young woman. Some technical and script problems keep it from really taking off.

A fashion photographer comes across a girl in a massage parlour that he thinks could be a knockout high-fashion model. He talks her into showing up for a test shooting at his studio. Soon after, she is introduced to the art of bondage and discipline, where she dresses up in leather and abuses men. She does such a good job that she quickly becomes famous as a dominatrix. But this life-style soon catches up to her.

The sex is quite kinky, filled with quasi-torture and humiliation. The murky photography gives a feeling of authenticity, but it is not especially erotic.

While she is a good erotic performer, Samantha Fox is not convincing as a model. She's a little hefty with chipmunk cheeks. References to her as "the most beautiful model in years" come off more humorous than accurate.

Genre: Graphic
Year: 1979
Time: 80 min.
Acting: Fair
Casting: Poor

Script: Fair
Production: Fair
Directing: Fair
Theme: Models
Humor: No

★ Watchable   ★★★ Must See
★★ Recommended   ★★★★ Masterpiece

H

HIGH SCHOOL FANTASIES ★★

Director: Morris Deal
Cast: Rene Bond, Rick Lutze, Tony Mazziotti, Nicole Riddell, Cindy Taylor, April Grant

This is a better-than-average pioneer adult film. It was one of the first to use the teen plot-line in an adult sex comedy, and was quite successful at it. The acting is not remarkable nor are the production values. Given the year it was made, however—and that nature of the adult-film industry—it was much better than most other films.

The story is about the kids of Zuni High. The plot spins off a stereotype called Freddy the Wimp and his desire to end his days as a virgin. The object of his lust is Mary Lou, the "pass-around cheerleader," played by Rene Bond. Freddy happens across a batch of Spanish Fly, and suddenly all the girls are after him.

The film portrays sex as a forbidden mystery, which is in keeping with its '50s period. It doesn't force the more typical adult formulas, but keeps to the type of sexual experiences common to young adults. There is a lot of necking, petting, and a touch of lesbianism. There is a sexually aggressive female teacher, a latent homosexual instructor, and an abundance of willing young girls.

The film is charming and often nostalgic, with pleasant music.

Genre: Graphic
Year: 1974
Time: 71 min.
Acting: Fair
Casting: Good

Script: Good
Production: Good
Directing: Good
Theme: Cheerleaders
Humor: Yes

HIGH SCHOOL MEMORIES ★

Directors: Anthony Spinelli and Godfrey Daniels
Cast: Annette Haven, Jamie Gillis, Chris Hopkins, John Leslie, Dorothy LeMay

Despite its high production values, an all-star cast, and two noted adult-film directors, this film is just too choppy and silly—and the actors are too old to be convincing as high school students. Also, Annette Haven is cast as the cheerleading coach and she looks younger and prettier than the cheerleaders. It was a good try, but only came out average.

The story is twofold. Part of it covers a football team traveling to a rival city for a game. The cheerleaders are so rambunctious and the coach so lascivious that the football team wears itself out with sexual activity before the game. They lose, and the coach is fired. The second part covers a five-year reunion where the cheerleaders, players, and coaches get together at a bar to talk about old times.

Many of the sexual situations are just silly and not erotic. The exceptions are Chris Hopkins' scenes, which are really exciting, and the final encounter between Annette Haven and Jamie Gillis, which is quite tender. Otherwise, the sex is common adult fare laced with poor humor and standard photography.

Genre: Graphic	**Script:** Poor
Year: 1981	**Production:** Good
Time: 94 min.	**Directing:** Fair
Acting: Fair	**Theme:** Cheerleaders
Casting: Fair	**Humor:** Yes

★ Watchable   ★★★ Must See
★★ Recommended   ★★★★ Masterpiece

H

JOHN HOLMES   aka Johnny Wadd

John Holmes is one of the most prolific actors in adult cinema. His long and distinguished career has been cut short, however, by some legal difficulties. He has recently been found innocent of the July 1, 1981 Laurel Canyon murders, but as of this writing is still being held by authorities for his possible involvement in a burglary ring.

Mr. Holmes is a graduate of UCLA, with a major in Physical Education. He got involved in erotic films when one of his girl friends suggested he talk to an adult film maker.

While his acting talents are not spectacular, his love-making capabilities are lengendary. He has appeared in hundreds of films, the most notable being: Autobiography of a Flea, The Erotic Adventures of Candy, Eruption, Hard Soap, Hard Soap, Prisoner of Paradise, Sweet Captive, and Exhausted. He is also known for his Johnny Wadd detective films, of which Blonde Fire is the most representative.

The recent film Exhausted is a straight-forward documentary on the life-style and career of this giant in adult cinema.

HONEYPIE ★

Director: Howard Ziehm
Cast: Jennifer Welles, Serena, Sharon Thorpe, Victoria Pagan, Terri Hall, Bree Anthony, Al Goldstein, Annie Sprinkle

The adult film industry is noted for its one-day wonders, films that are shot during the space of a single day. While this film might not have been shot in one day, it has that feel. The framing plot was shot quickly and the individual "stories" were pulled from other productions. Nevertheless, it is a film with some merit and is quite enticing as an adult film.

It is a vignette picture, and stories are framed by a simple plot involving the staff of a swinger's magazine. The readers send in letters and the editors read them aloud. The film then cuts to the episodes in pulsating, live action. One incident includes an older lady seducing a younger man. Another is about a female having an affair with two construction workers at the same time, and another handles some fairly intense bondage.

The sexual episodes are standard variations of the main adult themes: lesbian, leather, threesomes, etc. What makes this movie stand out is the sheer intensity and length of the erotic scenes. Sometimes it is quite compelling, often it is just tedious.

The film has a cameo appearance by Al Goldstein, the famous New York publisher of the controversial magazine *Screw*. He plays himself.

Genre: Graphic
Year: 1975
Time: 86 min.
Acting: Fair
Casting: Fair

Script: Poor
Production: Poor
Directing: Poor
Theme: Editors
Humor: Yes

★ Watchable   ★★★ Must See
★★ Recommended   ★★★★ Masterpiece

H

HOT AND SAUCY PIZZA GIRLS ★

Producer/director: Damon Christian
Cast: John Holmes, Desiree Cousteau, John Seeman, Laurien
Dominique, Candida Royalle, Christine DeShaffer

This is another Damon Christian light comedy, with some
fairly clever aspects. It is not very well made technically, but
it is charming in its raw, unpolished approach. The girls are
delightful, especially the constantly dizzy Desiree Cousteau.
   The film is about an ailing pizzeria. To boost sales, the
owner decides to hire only pretty girls to deliver pizza. Then
he decides to sell the girls as well, or at least rent them. He
starts San Francisco's only call-girl/pizza-delivery business,
and quite quickly becomes successful. But, the fried chicken
establishments don't like the competition, so they hire a giant,
mad chicken to hassle the delivery girls.
   The sexual scenes are quite gratuitous, but fun all the same.
On the whole, the film is quite silly, dimly photographed, and
often uneven in its plotting.

Genre: Graphic
Year: 1978
Time: 71 min.
Acting: Poor
Casting: Good

Script: Fair
Production: Fair
Directing: Poor
Theme: Waitresses
Humor: Yes

HOT DALLAS NIGHTS ★★½

Producer: Julian Orynski
Director: Tony Kendrick
Cast: Hillary Summers, Raven Turner, R. J. Reynolds,
Alexander Kingsford, Tara Flynn

Television has always been a great source for parody in adult films, and this one does a comic takeoff of the popular series, *Dallas*. It has some clever humor, and a convoluted plot line with thoroughly indulgent characters.

It is about the Brewing family and their attempt to corner the market in fertilizers. The two brothers do some dirty dealing with the competition and with each other's wives. Meanwhile, Duke is hired to help out around the ranch, and when the two lascivious brothers are away, he begins seducing the Brewing women himself. When the two brothers are found trying to burn another company's warehouse, trouble follows.

The sexual encounters are quite hilarious. One of the Brewing brothers is a cowboy fanatic, riding his women like horses, wearing only leather boots and spurs.

For an adult film, the comedy is quite effective and well-executed. This spoof is filled with belly laughs, double entendres, and some of the worst over-acting you ever laughed through.

Genre: Graphic
Year: 1981
Time: 83 min.
Acting: Good
Casting: Good

Script: Fair
Production: Good
Directing: Fair
Theme: Cowgirls
Humor: Yes

★ Watchable ★★★ Must See
★★ Recommended ★★★★ Masterpiece

H

HOT RACKETS ★½

Producer: Sam Norvell
Director: Robert McCallum
Cast: Candida Royalle, Jon Martin, Laurien Dominique, Rhonda Jo Petty, Mike Fairmont

When this movie first came out, it was promoted as a big-budget, top-notch adult film, and received some fairly good reviews. Though it never really worked theatrically, it seems to have found an audience in the videocassette market. It does have superior production values, pretty girls, and a number of erotic situations, but the ending is disappointing.

The story is about a rich couple who are having sexual difficulties with each other and go to an exclusive tennis resort to work out their problems. It is no ordinary tennis club, but one that caters to a bunch of lascivious, high-society swingers.

The sex scenes are exciting, but a bit long. The confrontation between Laurien Dominique and Candida Royalle in the steam room is exceptional. The rest of the film is fairly standard adult fare.

Though the cinematography is good, the plotting is too loose, and the film bores near the end.

Genre: Graphic
Year: 1979
Time: 90 min.
Acting: Fair
Casting: Good

Script: Fair
Production: Very good
Directing: Good
Theme: Swinging Couples
Humor: Yes

I AM CURIOUS—YELLOW ★★

Director: Vilgot Sjöman
Photographer: Peter Wester
Cast: Lena Nyman, Börje Ahlstedt, Peter Lindgren,
   Gunnel Bröstrom

In the sixties, the Swedish films were known to be the most sexually graphic, but this is the one that really rocked the world. It was shocking in its uninhibited portrayal of sex and in its diatribe of social democracy. It was a significant step forward in getting the adult film shown in the theaters.

The film comes in two editions, blue and yellow. The blue version focuses more on the political issues and the yellow concentrates on the emergence of sexual liberation. The lead character is a young Swedish girl who attempts to cling to her philosophy of nonviolence, free love, and democratic socialism. But the realities of her life force her to adopt new and broader ideologies.

I Am Curious–Yellow was the first major release to show full frontal nudity of both male and female performers, and genuine intercourse on screen. Strangely enough, in Sweden it was criticized more for its left-wing attitudes than for its courageous display of sex.

Genre: Erotic
Year: 1967
Time: 121 min.
Acting: Very Good
Casting: Good

Script: Good
Production: Very Good
Directing: Very Good
Theme: Young Girl
Humor: Yes

★ Watchable   ★★★ Must See
★★ Recommended   ★★★★ Masterpiece

I

I LOVE YOU ★★★½

Producer: Walter Clark
Director: Arnaldo Jabor
Cast: Sonia Braga, Paulo C. Pereio, Tarcisio Meira,
   Vera Fischer

This is a wonderful little film from Brazil. The acting, especially by Sonia Braga, is outstanding. The film is quite sensual, revealing, comic, even at times tragic. It should play well in many of the art threaters across the country.

The story is quite simple, transparent even. A member of the Brazilian upper-class has a bra factory that just went bankrupt and a beautiful blonde wife that just left him. He wallows in self-pity in his expensive penthouse apartment. He finally goes out, gets drunk, and ends up in the middle of a lover's quarrel. He asks the woman in the quarrel to come up to his place, and surprisingly she accepts. She pretends to be a whore, and a comic repartee ensues, ending in a boldly erotic affair.

For a mainstream film, the sexual encounters are quite graphic, but do not linger. Instead, the scenes are shot from a distance, swiftly and teasingly, with numerous close-ups of the lovers' faces writhing in ecstasy and quasi-humorous screaming.

The cinematography is appealing, colorful, and contains a lot of black space for effect. It creates a world filled with shadows and only an occasional bright spot. The bedroom, of course, is bathed in golden light.

I Love You is a warm, friendly film that takes its time developing its view of the erotic attraction between the sexes.

Genre: Erotic	**Script:** Very Good
Year: 1982	**Production:** Very Good
Time: 102 min.	**Directing:** Very Good
Acting: Excellent	**Theme:** Lost Love
Casting: Excellent	**Humor:** Yes

ILSA, SHE WOLF OF THE SS ★

Director: Don Edmonds
Cast: Dyanne Thorne, Greg Knoph, Sandi Richman

This is one of the few films that has attempted to combine strong sex with graphic gore, blood, and physical mutilations.

The setting is a Nazi concentration camp. In the medical building, Ilsa is supervising heinous sex experiments. She picks one male prisoner to spend the night with her, and if he satisfies her, she keeps him. If not, he is castrated and put back into the medical ward for further "experiments." One young man survives the test, and after gaining the confidence of Ilsa, plots his escape and final revenge.

The treatment of sex is revolting. This is intentional. Graphic mutilations are displayed with general lack of taste, juxtaposed against potent sexual activity. Fortunately, however, the film is so badly made that much of the power that could have been generated is lost.

The busty Dyanne Thorne is a convincing Nazi devil, and is able to bring out an eerie combination of beauty, power, and evil.

Genre: Taboo
Year: 1974
Time: 95 min.
Acting: Fair
Casting: Good

Script: Poor
Production: Fair
Directing: Fair
Theme: Torture, Sex Experiments
Humor: No

★ Watchable ★★★ Must See
★★ Recommended ★★★★ Masterpiece

I

THE IMMORAL MR. TEAS ★

Producer: Peter A. Decenzie
Director: Russ Meyer
Narration: Edward J. Lakso
Cast: Bill Teas, Ann Peters, Marilyn Wesley, Michelle Roberts, Dawn Danielle

This is Russ Meyer's first venture into titillating adult films. For 1959, it was a big sensation. By today's standards, however, it is quite tame. It is a difficult film to rate because it is so delightful and adorable, but the story is almost nonexistent and certainly dated.

The story is about a dirty-minded voyeur. Through the course of a day, he sees a number of good-looking, big-breasted ladies, and ogles them for long periods of time. On the weekend, he goes to the beach where he comes across a photographer and a topless model.

Russ Meyer was very careful not to place his characters in sexual situations, but concentrated on titillating the audience. Mr. Teas finds himself with a nude female analyst, for example, but does not try to seduce her.

Such tease was a matter of the film's survival. For the very moment nudity turned into a sexual encounter, it would have certainly been censored. It pushed nudity to the limit of the time and was significant in laying ground for future adult films.

Genre: Erotic	**Script:** Fair
Year: 1959	**Production:** Good
Time: 63 min.	**Directing:** Good
Acting: Fair	**Theme:** Chesty Ladies
Casting: Fair	**Humor:** Yes

INDECENT EXPOSURE ★

Producer: Harold Lime
Director: Robert McCallum
Cast: Veronica Hart, Jesie St. James, Richard Bolla

Despite some rather nice cinematography and sensual performances, the script of this recent Harold Lime production is so oddly patched together that the film fails to merit a higher rating.

Tony is a very successful fashion photographer, but he's getting very bored with his job. He decides to go on a photo tour and do a pictorial study of the typical, all-American high school girl. He takes along his two attractive assistants, Lyla and June. He also invites one of his old buddies, Ted, along for the ride. Off they go, photographing beautiful young women with much fanfare and sensual indulgence.

The sex is varied and sometimes fun. It is, in fact, the film's biggest asset. The scene where Eric Edwards seduces the exotic Arcadia Lake is very effective and the ending sequence, while it is out of context with the rest of the film, is filled with offbeat eroticism, including bondage, threesomes, and quasirape.

The film's weakest point is in the ballet sequence, where it is ridiculously obvious that the ballerinas are untrained and turn out to be horrible dancers.

Despite its inadequacies, the film is becoming very popular in the videocassette scene. This may be due to the appearances of the adorable Veronica Hart and Jesie St. James.

Genre: Graphic	**Script:** Poor
Year: 1981	**Production:** Very Good
Time: 85 min.	**Directing:** Fair
Acting: Fair	**Theme:** Models, Ballerinas
Casting: Fair	**Humor:** Yes

★ Watchable	★★★ Must See
★★ Recommended	★★★★ Masterpiece

I

INSATIABLE

Director: Godfrey Daniels
Cast: Marilyn Chambers, John Holmes, Jesie St. James

This film marks Marilyn Chambers' return to the adult screen after four years of trying a career in dreadful horror movies and the live stage in Las Vegas. It is a lushly produced film, with some good settings and a number of superior erotic performances.

The story centers around a glamorous fashion model named Sandra (Marilyn Chambers). Her parents suffer an auto accident, leaving Sandra with an incredible fortune and estate. She has everything she needs: money, cars, house, etc. But she is consumed with erotic fantasies, and can't get enough.

There are actually few sex scenes in this movie, but each one is masterfully crafted. The film doesn't catalog every erotic variation, but it does have a very soft lesbian affair, a quasi-rape on a pool table, and a voyeuristic fantasy as Sandra watches her best friend make love.

The cinematography is superior for an adult film, with some beautiful sets, fantasy sequences, and outdoor locations. The story and acting, however, sometimes dip into sentimentalism and the plot folds back onto itself for no reason. The picture's strong point is in the personality of Ms. Chambers, who is exquisite and charming on screen.

Genre: Graphic	**Script:** Fair
Year: 1980	**Production:** Very Good
Time: 80 min.	**Directing:** Good
Acting: Fair	**Theme:** Model
Casting: Good	**Humor:** No

I

INSIDE DESIREE COUSTEAU ★

Director: Leon Gucci
Cast: Desiree Cousteau, John Holmes, Serena

When actresses achieve some sort of fame in the adult industry, they always seem to do an "inside" film. This one has nothing remarkable about it except that Desiree Cousteau is so exotically dizzy that almost everything she does is charming.

The movie is a fictionalized account of Desiree's rise to stardom in the adult-film industry. Job after job, she is mistreated, seduced, almost raped a time or two, but basically always seems to end up as some man's sex toy. So she decides to cash in on her lascivious talents and get into sex films, where she comes to fame and glory.

The erotic encounters are quite standard, but Desiree's off-the-wall screen presence is so alluring that we always feel drawn into her misadventures. She's cute, innocent, scatterbrained, and erotically curious.

As an adult film, it caters solely to fans of Miss Cousteau and offers little else.

Genre: Graphic
Year: 1980
Time: 90 min.
Acting: Fair
Casting: Good

Script: Poor
Production: Fair
Directing: Poor
Theme: Desiree Cousteau
Humor: Yes

★ Watchable   ★★★ Must See
★★ Recommended   ★★★★ Masterpiece

I

INSIDE JENNIFER WELLES ★

Producer: Howard A. Howard
Director: Jennifer Welles
Cast: Jennifer Welles, Richard Bolla, Marlene Willoughby, Cheri Baines, Dave Ruby

This was one of the first of the "inside" films, and is no better or worse than most of the others of similar intention. It is quite long, but some of the erotic encounters are very well done.

This film is not about Jennifer Welles' rise to stardom, but simply her reminiscences about her first sexual experiences. She begins by describing to the audience the circumstances, then the screen dissolves into a film re-creation of the event.

Her first lesbian encounter is quite nicely done, and the seductress is well-played by Marlene Willoughby. But the film's best scene is near the end, where Miss Welles takes on nine young men at the same time.

Jennifer Welles did very few films, though her following has persisted long after her retirement from adult films. For her fans, this film will undoubtedly be appealing, but to most people, it will be long and quite uneventful.

Genre: Graphic
Year: 1977
Time: 118 min.
Acting: Good
Casting: Fair

Script: Poor
Production: Fair
Directing: Poor
Theme: Jennifer Welles
Humor: No

INSIDE MARILYN CHAMBERS ★★½

Directors: Mitchell Brothers
Cast: Marilyn Chambers, Johnnie Keyes, George S. McDonald

This is a fairly accurate documentary on the life of Marilyn Chambers, star of *Behind the Green Door* and *The Resurrection of Eve*.

It begins with an on-camera interview with Marilyn in which she talks about her past (including her time as an Ivory Snow detergent model) and how she got into adult films. Despite its antiquated techniques (the narration is a throwback to the fifties), the information comes across clearly. For those who are interested in this charming lady, the film is enlightening and quite exciting.

There are clips from her famous films and a lot of cuts to her graphic sex scenes. Outtakes from her early films show Marilyn looking upset with what she's doing, but such clips tend to heighten the realism.

Also interviewed are Johnnie Keyes, ex-boxer, and George S. McDonald, adult-film actor. Both talk about Chambers and their participation with her in her films.

Genre: Graphic	**Script:** Fair
Year: 1975	**Production:** Good
Time: 75 min.	**Directing:** Good
Acting: Good	**Theme:** Marilyn Chambers
Casting: Excellent	**Humor:** No

★	Watchable	★★★	Must See
★★	Recommended	★★★★	Masterpiece

I

INSIDE SEKA

Producer: Howard A. Howard
Directors: Seka and Ken Yontz
Cast: Seka, Ken Yontz, Christie Ford, Merle Michaels, Ron Jeremy, Ron Hudd, Roy Stuard

Like *Inside Desiree Cousteau* this film is ranked among the top adult films because of the large appeal of its lead actress, Seka. She is an exotic, platinum blonde with a large adult following, but unfortunately this film does not meet the standards of many of her other productions, nor does it favorably compare with other pseudo-documentaries.

The movie is about Seka and her live-in boyfriend, Ken, and their swinging life-style. Those who know Seka and Ken say that many of the incidents in the film are based on fact, but one can reasonably assume that they have been greatly exaggerated and enhanced.

All the same, Seka is an adequate erotic performer, though her talents as an actress aren't enormous. She always brings to the screen a strong sense of evil pleasure. Her wanton lust and exotic beauty, coupled with a compelling thirst for explicit sexual adventure, make her a very popular adult cinema star.

For those who have reservations about Seka, however, the film should be avoided.

Genre: Graphic	**Script:** Poor
Year: 1980	**Production:** Poor
Time: 96 min.	**Directing:** Fair
Acting: Poor	**Theme:** Seka
Casting: Fair	**Humor:** No

IN THE REALM OF THE SENSES ★★★

Director: Nagisa Oshima
Cast: Eiko Matsuda, Tatsuya Fuji

This is a film that is so wonderfully plotted and expertly acted that it almost has a dream-like effect. It's an erotic fantasy turned nightmare.

It is the story of a sexual relationship between a young Japanese couple. At first lustful and erotic, they can't get enough. However, their experiments in sensationalism end in tragedy.

The film is spiced with strange yet genuinely humorous moments. For example, an older lady chances upon the lovers, and—for the fun of it—the young man initiates a ménage à trois. The incident proves to be so exhilarating that the old woman dies from exhaustion. The scene is played with such verve and intensity that—despite the fatal outcome—it does have a strange humorous overtone to it.

Oshima developed with great care all the minor details of this affair without ever becoming overbearing or didactic. It is one of the most gripping films to have ever handled sexual obsession.

Genre: Erotic
Year: 1979
Time: 104 min.
Acting: Excellent
Casting: Excellent

Script: Very Good
Production: Very Good
Directing: Very Good
Theme: Erotic Obsession
Humor: Yes

★ Watchable ★★★ Must See
★★ Recommended ★★★★ Masterpiece

I

IT HAPPENED IN HOLLYWOOD ★★★

Producers: Jim Buckley and *Screw Magazine*
Director: Peter Locke
Cast: Felicity Split, Harry Reems, Marc Stevens, Peter
Bramley, Al Goldstein

According to a recent interview with Harry Reems, right after
the success of *Deep Throat* everyone wanted to do zany sex
comedies. This film is an excellent example. It is wacky,
high-spirited, fun, and very raunchy. It's a little dated, but
still holds up a decade later.

A bored phone operator dreams of becoming a sex star, and
when she loses her job, she decides to take up the quest. She
sets out and enters the world of kooky, underground filmmakers. It is one of the funniest, raunchiest, most hilarious
couplings of off-the-wall sex and slapstick around. Everyone
in the film is literally out of his mind.

The film follows the pattern set by *Deep Throat,* but improves upon the basic design. The sex scenes are fast-paced,
filled with belly laughs and a lot of dirty jokes. It is loads of
fun for those with the proper minds. It is not for the
squeamish.

Genre: Graphic
Year: 1973
Time: 74 min.
Acting: Good
Casting: Good

Script: Very Good
Production: Good
Directing: Very Good
Theme: Telephone Operator
Humor: Yes

J

JACK 'N JILL ★★

Producer: Felix Miguel Arroyo
Director: Mark Ubell
Cast: Samantha Fox, Jack Wrangler, Eric Edwards, Vanessa Del Rio, Rikki O'Neal

This is a very solid adult film. It's witty, funny, and very sexy, ranking above the average.

It is about a couple named, obviously, Jack and Jill. While they like each other, they are getting quite bored with life in general and decide to start playing some games on their friends. The first one involves an innocent round of strip poker, but soon turns into something more provocative. Having had a taste of swinging, they decide to answer a couple of ads in the swinger's guides.

A lot of eroticism is quite heated and usually involves pairs of couples together. Samantha Fox gives one of her best performances.

The story is cute and helps to tie the major scenes together, but it is, like most adult movies, subordinate to much of the gratuitous sexual activity.

Genre: Graphic
Year: 1979
Time: 75 min.
Acting: Good
Casting: Good

Script: Good
Production: Good
Directing: Fair
Theme: Swinging Couples
Humor: Yes

★ Watchable   ★★★ Must See
★★ Recommended   ★★★★ Masterpiece

J

THE JOY OF LETTING GO

Producer: Summer Brown
Director: John Gregory
Cast: Dominique St. Pierre, Clint Hughes, Susan Sun Lee,
James Kral, Constance Money

This is a typical adult film, but some of the action and erotic
sequences are worthy of being singled out. The production
values are fairly good, the acting is somewhat realistic, and
the treatment of women is quite soft and sensual in many
scenes.

The story is a common one for adult films. A bored, rich
housewife experiments with prostitution for kicks. Of course,
she discovers that it is not her thing. She meets a high-class
pimp at a health club. He's charming and gracious and she has
a fling with him. But he turns mean and ugly when the question of money comes up, and he forces her onto the street.

The soft treatment of lesbianism is evidenced by the fact
that a woman, Summer Brown, is producing the film. But
many of the other forms of sex are downright mean, especially
when the pimp turns sour and kidnaps the woman's body-
guard. The housewife's three-day odyssey on the street is
shrouded in sleazy settings, repulsive clients, and loveless,
graphic sex.

On the whole, the film gets quite tedious in parts, but there
is enough action and erotic enticement to hold one's interest.

Genre: Graphic
Year: 1976
Time: 86 min.
Acting: Good
Casting: Fair

Script: Good
Production: Very Good
Directing: Good
Theme: Bored Housewife
Humor: No

JUSTINE ★★

Producer/director: Robert R. Walters
Cast: Hillary Summers, Vanessa Del Rio, Ashley Moore, Merle
Michaels, Christie Ford, Christine De Shaffer

A girl's coming of age and her first sexual encounter is a
highly charged moment, and many adult films have been
made about it. This one has lush production values and a cast
sprinkled with good looking, zesty girls.

Justine, having just graduated from a French finishing
school, decides to go live with her rich uncle. She is charming
and sweet, but her uncle is scandalous and wanton. While
living with him, Justine happens one day to enter her uncle's
bathroom and discovers him with his mistress. This utterly
shocks the innocent Justine, and she runs frightened to her
bedroom. The image of the sexual encounter burns in her
mind, however, and she begins to have lusty, sex-filled
dreams of her own.

For the bulk of the film, Justine is a virgin with explicit
fantasies. In the end, however, she strategically moves from
fantasy to reality. The film is well photographed, rich and
colorful, with some sensual acting by Summers and Del Rio.
Except for these two young actresses, though, the film really
doesn't stand apart from the mass of adult movies.

Genre: Graphic
Year: 1980
Time: 84 min.
Acting: Good
Casting: Fair

Script: Fair
Production: Very Good
Directing: Good
Theme: Virgin
Humor: No

| ★ Watchable | ★★★ Must See |
| ★★ Recommended | ★★★★ Masterpiece |

K

JOHNNIE KEYES

Johnnie Keyes got into the erotic film business almost by accident. After a very successful career as a boxer, he began to audition for a number of film roles. One of them was an erotic film by Artie and Jim Mitchell. At first Keyes didn't understand the full demands of the sexual role. But when he found out, he was delighted.

He was not originally cast in Behind the Green Door, but in another smaller role. When the shooting started, Mr. Keyes was involved in some minor legal difficulties, and was being held by authorities. The Mitchell brothers held up shooting for a couple of days, and recast him in the role that made him famous.

With the success of Behind the Green Door, Johnnie Keyes was thrust into the limelight along with Marilyn Chambers, and has since starred in The Resurrection of Eve, Heavenly Desire, Pro Ball Cheerleaders, Sex World, and Aunt Peg's Fulfillment.

Keyes is one of the very few black actors to have achieved stardom in adult films.

KINKY LADIES OF BOURBON STREET ★★

Director: Francis Leroi
Cast: Dawn Cummings, Helga Trixi, Penelope Lamour,
Veronique Monad

This is a very interesting French film with some better-than-average production values and some solid erotic performances.

Four very promiscuous ladies, who each have been caught in a compromising situation on the job, decide to commit suicide. They want to go the best way they can think of, which turns out to be sex-til-death. The girls shack up at a chateau and begin.

The film is wall-to-wall sex, graphic and explicit. One girl plays a bit too long with lighted dynamite, and goes out with a bang. Another takes on a working crew and dies of exhaustion. The third meets a lover who excites her to death. The last woman lives to tell the story.

The sets and cinematography are quite lush, and the story premise is a compelling one. Unfortunately, its development is too spotty and improbable to take seriously.

Genre: Graphic   **Script:** Fair
Year: 1977   **Production:** Good
Time: 87 min.   **Directing:** Good
Acting: Fair   **Theme:** Obsession
Casting: Good   **Humor:** No

| ★ Watchable | ★★★ Must See |
| ★★ Recommended | ★★★★ Masterpiece |

SYLVIA KRISTEL

Sylvia Kristel was born on September 29, 1952 in Utrecht, Holland. Her parents were staunch Calvinists and raised their daughter according to its discipline, but as a young girl Sylvia ran away from home for a less restricted life style. She supported herself by taking on a number of odd jobs: gas station attendant, a secretary, etc. She also started getting a few modeling jobs as well. Her elegant and attractive features soon made her quite successful in the profession, and by 1972 she had graduated into doing films.

She gained international recognition in 1974 for her sensual performance in Emmanuelle and went on to do Emmanuelle — The Joys of a Woman, Goodbye Emmanuelle, Alice or the Last Escapade, Rene la Canne, Mysteries, and Airport '79 Concorde. Her recent film Private Lessons has been very popular in the United States and has become something of a cult film. Sylvia has demonstrated some very sophisticated acting ability and her mysteriously sensual good looks have made her quite a popular actress. She is currently working in a lush film adaptation of D. H. Lawrence's Lady Chatterly's Lover.

LAST TANGO IN PARIS ★★★★

Director: Bernardo Bertolucci
Cast: Marlon Brando, Maria Schneider

When *Last Tango* appeared in 1973, it created quite a storm because of its bold subject matter and big-name personalities. Though many regarded it as the low point of the perverse and decadent trend in filmmaking, the film is actually a serious study of the sexual struggle of a guilt-ridden, lonely American in Paris. It is superbly crafted and the sexual electricity between Brando and Schneider is supercharged.

The film begins with the American looking for an apartment. He finds one, but a pretty young French girl wants it too. They argue, but the argument merely intensifies the obvious sexual attraction between them. They agree to share the apartment, but not names.

Their sexual bouts are very brutal and very animalistic. At one point, Brando tosses her to the floor and forces her to submit to some "Greek" lovemaking. For her, however, it's not love. It's just sex. And soon she can't take it any longer.

Films have handled this sort of subject matter before, but not in quite the same way. To some, it may be shocking in its frank approach to offbeat sexual relationships.

Genre: Erotic
Year: 1973
Time: 132 min.
Acting: Excellent
Casting: Excellent

Script: Excellent
Production: Excellent
Directing: Excellent
Theme: Mid-Life Crisis
Humor: No

★ Watchable   ★★★ Must See
★★ Recommended   ★★★★ Masterpiece

L

THE LEGEND OF LADY BLUE ★★

Director: A. Fabritzi
Cast: Maureen Spring, John Smith, Obe-Wahn, Gloria
Leonard, Faye Young

Despite the fact that this film won the AFAA's best picture award, it is barely better than most adult pictures. The acting is passable to poor. The story is underdeveloped and much of the dialogue is weak, but it does have some great sexual encounters, including an exotic brothel sequence.

The film is about the sexual awakening of two small-town boys. To them, sex is still a great mystery and they decide to go out and find out about it.

The film follows their erotic adventures in a glowing, uninhibited style. One of the surprising aspects is the inclusion of Vietnam War footage, specifically a moldy, Southeast Asian brothel. This sequence is really a treat.

On the whole, however, the film is uneven, the story insubstantial and convoluted.

Genre: Graphic
Year: 1979
Time: 88 min.
Acting: Poor
Casting: Fair

Script: Poor
Production: Good
Directing: Fair
Theme: Sexual Awakening
Humor: No

★ Watchable   ★★★ Must See
★★ Recommended   ★★★★ Masterpiece

JOHN LESLIE

Even before getting involved in erotic films, John Leslie had been an entertainer. As a young man, he participated in a number of summer theaters, tried his hand at being a painter, and organized a band that played together for over five years.

In 1975 he met some people in San Francisco who suggested that he audition for adult film roles. His first two films were Coming Attractions and Night Pleasure, a couple of minor films, but effective in displaying his talents as an actor. Three years later, he won the Erotica Award for Best Supporting Actor in A Coming of Angels. Recently, he has won the Erotica for Best Actor two years in a row, for Talk Dirty To Me (1981) and Wicked Sensations (1982).

His favorite film, however, has been the highly acclaimed Nothing To Hide. Other films he has starred in are: Exposed, "F," High School Memories, Insatiable, The Other Side of Julie, Shoppe of Temptations, V—The Hot One, The Dancers, Outlaw Ladies, and A Thousand and One Erotic Nights.

John Leslie still lives in San Francisco and is very active in the adult-film business.

L

LIPPS & McCAIN

Producer: Damon Christian
Director: Bob Chinn
Cast: Paul Thomas, Rick Lutz, Amber Hunt, Pat Rhea,
   Vicki Lindsay

Typical of the Damon Christian films, this one is delightfully silly, but a lot of fun. The production values are elaborate for such a low-budget film. Some of the acting is good, and many of the erotic encounters are well-motivated, which offers some room for laughs.

It is the story of two modern young men who refuse to grow out of their nineteenth-century cowboy fantasies. They come across a ranch and quickly talk the father and his two sons into a game of poker. While McCain is playing with the men, Lipps is out in the barn playing with the daughter. A forced retreat into the desert leads them into encounters with a motorcycle gang, a couple of mafia hit men, and other weird stuff.

The sex is fun, indulgent, and very erotic. It is of the nothing-is-left-to-the-imagination variety, but still quite teasing in its approach. It's a little sophomoric, but fun to watch, nonetheless.

Genre: Graphic
Year: 1978
Time: 95 min.
Acting: Fair
Casting: Good

Script: Fair
Production: Good
Directing: Good
Theme: Cowboys
Humor: Yes

LITTLE DARLINGS ★

Director: Jim Clark
Cast: Lysa Thatcher, Richard Bolla, Lori Palmer

The best thing going for this film are the young girls. Many adult movies cast girls who are just too old-looking. However, young girls alone do not a movie make.

A vanload of teenage girls breaks down en route to summer camp. They spend the night at a nearby resort while a local mechanic fixes the van. The desk clerk (Richard Bolla) turns out to be a wolf and begins seducing a number of the girls while trying to fend off his female tyrant of a boss.

The girls are perky and pubescent with a sense of innocence, especially Lysa Thatcher. She is curious about her sexuality and experiments with some of the other girls and the hotel clerk, where she learns a few new tricks. The treatment of sex is basically run-of-the-mill—lesbian, threesomes, cute-but-compromising situations, etc.

Lori Palmer shines in her devious role as the feisty hotel owner and Richard Bolla brings off an adequate performance.

Genre: Graphic
Year: 1981
Time: 84 min.
Acting: Fair
Casting: Very Good

Script: Fair
Production: Good
Directing: Fair
Theme: Schoolgirls
Humor: Yes

★ Watchable ★★★ Must See
★★ Recommended ★★★★ Masterpiece

L

THE LITTLE FRENCH MAID

Director: Adele Robbins
Cast: Connie Peters, John Holmes, Paul Thomas

This standard adult film employs good production values. A young French girl is hired as a maid to work at a posh estate. As it turns out, both the butler and the master of the house have some very demanding chores for the maid to carry out (hint: it's not dusting). The maid, however, is not upset by the lascivious demands. In fact, she likes them and goes outside the household for more.

She narrates the story as if it were an insightful study into the secret erotic life of someone important, but the story never goes anywhere, nor does it uncover any unique character traits or insights.

The sex is filled with quick set-ups into heavy action sequences. The maid is ordered by the master to perform for him, and she does so with the enthusiasm of most sex stars.

Genre: Graphic
Year: 1981
Time: 90 min.
Acting: Poor
Casting: Poor

Script: Poor
Production: Good
Directing: Fair
Theme: Maids
Humor: No

LITTLE GIRLS BLUE ★★

Director: Joanna Williams
Cast: Tamara Morgan, Kristine Heller, Elaine Wells

Ah, the classic schoolgirl adult film, simple and fun. The story centers on the erotic fantasies and exploits of a group of uniformed teenage girls attending an exclusive girls' school. To get a better grade, one girl seduces her teacher. Another, fearing math, plays out an erotic fantasy where she shrinks into a pad of paper and solves life-size mathematical problems while carrying on a sexual episode with the instructor.

The erotic scenes feature great photography and sets, giving the film a high-budget look (finances actually were meager). The most prevalent form of sexual excitation for the girls seems to be an obsession with oral exams, but the film is filled with a wide variety of erotic delights.

On the whole, the film never really develops, but the bits and pieces are quite exciting.

Genre: Graphic
Year: 1978
Time: 90 min.
Acting: Fair
Casting: Good

Script: Fair
Production: Very Good
Directing: Good
Theme: Schoolgirls
Humor: Yes

★ Watchable   ★★★ Must See
★★ Recommended   ★★★★ Masterpiece

L

LORNA ★½

Director: Russ Meyer
Cast: Lorna Maitland, James Rucker, Hal Hopper

With *The Immoral Mr. Teas*, Russ Meyer was one of the pioneers of sex films. He knew, however, that the country would eventually want more than just naked ladies romping around the countryside, and went for a strong plot that contained a well-motivated but heavy sex scene.

Lorna is a frustrated housewife. She lives in a dilapidated riverside shack with a deadbeat but sweet husband. He works hard all day and studies all night, leaving her unfulfilled. One day, while the husband is at work, an escaped convict bursts in on Lorna and rapes her. She is so enraptured by the experience that she becomes infatuated with him, but when her husband unexpectedly returns from work, she doesn't know what to do.

Lorna was one of the first films to show nudity in the context of strong sex. While there was nothing really explicit or graphic about it, it was truly shocking for its time. Today, however, it is quite tame. The story borders on melodrama and many of the plot points are too convenient to be taken seriously.

Genre: Erotic
Year: 1964
Time: 78 min.
Acting: Good
Casting: Very Good

Script: Good
Production: Good
Directing: Very Good
Theme: Housewife
Humor: Yes

MADAM KITTY (SALON KITTY) ★★½

Director: Biovanni Tinto Brass
Cast: Helmut Berger, Ingrid Thulin, Teresa Ann Savoy

Madam Kitty is a part exploitation, part serious study of Nazi atrocities. It actually has a lot of merit as a film, but its story is uneven.

Kitty Kellermann runs a brothel that caters to the German elite. Unknown to her, it has been bugged by a top SS officer to gain incriminating evidence against some of Germany's top brass. One of the girls, Margherita, falls in love with a German officer who wants to defect to the Allies. The plot is discovered, and Margherita is used as an informer, but when she tells Madam Kitty about the goings-on in her house, she is outraged and plots revenge.

The film indulges in many of the perversions and sexual humiliations the Germans inflicted on the whores of Salon Kitty. Tinto Brass directs the film with a heavy hand, zooming constantly during the ending sequence to create a hypnotic effect. He doesn't shy away from the atrocities, and often revels in them. The characterizations are very solid and realistic, but the movie's harsh portrayal of much of the sexual activity has kept it out of the mainstream.

Genre: Erotic
Year: 1976
Time: 129 min.
Acting: Good
Casting: Good

Script: Good
Production: Very Good
Directing: Good
Theme: Brothel, Nazis
Humor: Yes

★ Watchable   ★★★ Must See
★★ Recommended   ★★★★ Masterpiece

M

MAITRESSE

Director: Barbet Schroeder
Cast: Gerard Depardieu, Bulle Ogier, Andre Rouyer

This film met some pretty stiff reviews when it first appeared in France. It was different, unsettling, and quite realistic. But since then, it has developed a cult following in many U.S. art theaters.

A young man, Oliver, arrives in Paris and is quickly caught up in a burglary ring with a friend named Mario. While casing a place, a young woman, Ariane, tells the boys of a likely apartment that happens to be right beneath her own. When they enter, they find it filled with torture equipment, whips, chains, racks, and even a man in a cage.

Oliver and Mario are both curious and uncomfortable with the setting, but Ariane, having changed into an all-leather outfit, bolts the door and forces the boys to undergo a series of sexual humiliations. The next day, Oliver happens to see Ariane, and she's "normal" again. She denies any misdoing. Oliver becomes so intrigued with her dual life that he gets involved romantically with her, which turns out to be a mistake.

The acting is believable and the reactions to the beatings and humiliation quite genuine. In fact, Schroeder cast an actual dominatrix to double for Ariane's role, complete with some of her actual clients. Despite its approach, the film does not linger needlessly on its sexual perversions, nor does it exploit the torture. Schroeder approaches it from the character point of view, studying the dual nature of a bizarre woman.

Genre: Taboo
Year: 1976
Time: 112 min.
Acting: Very Good
Casting: Excellent

Script: Good
Production: Very Good
Directing: Very Good
Theme: Dominate Women, Leather
Humor: Not Really

MARASCHINO CHERRY ★★

Producer: Morton Breman
Director: Henry Paris (Radley Metzger)
Cast: Gloria Leonard, Jenny Baxter, Constance Money, Lesllie Bovèe, Annette Haven, C.J. Laing

While this film has a fairly standard adult plot, director Henry Paris has a way of making something trite sparkle. And this film does sparkle. It also contains some interesting sex and some good acting.

The story is about a young, country girl coming to the big city. Her older sister, Maraschino, turns out to be a madam at a cathouse. The younger sister, however, is not repulsed, but highly intrigued. Maraschino offers to teach her little sibling the ropes.

There is an abundance of sexual situations in this film, with the interesting appearance of a mild bondage sequence. The scene is neither humorous nor seriously painful, but quite erotic. The lesbian encounters tend to become overlong, and there is a lot of application of love aids, giving the audience a rich variety of stimulating situations.

Genre: Graphic
Year: 1978
Time: 83 min.
Acting: Good
Casting: Good

Script: Fair
Production: Very Good
Directing: Good
Theme: Cathouse
Humor: Yes

★ Watchable ★★★ Must See
★★ Recommended ★★★★ Masterpiece

M

WILLIAM MARGOLD

Before his involvement in adult films, Margold was a parole officer who also dabbled in writing. While working on a story about nude modeling, he found a small, ailing agency and helped to get it rolling again. He soon became involved with it full time, and found himself in leading adult film roles.

Margold has an uncanny ability to get involved with extremely sleazy, low-budget, often brutal and anti-feminine films, his most notable being the sadistic comedy Weekend Fantasy. He has also played in Marilyn and the Senator; Olympic Fever; Plato's, The Movie; The Masters & Ms. Johnson; Ring of Desire; and Fantasm Comes Again.

As an agent, he helped establish Seka in adult films. His current lover/protege is the stunning brunette Drea, who is currently gaining a lot of respect as an erotic performer. He has also been a very close friend of the notable Serena for over eight years. They have adopted each other as brother and sister.

M

MARY! MARY! ★★★

Producer/director/writer: Bernard Morris
Cast: Constance Money, John Leslie, Sharon Thorpe, Jon Martin, Sandy Penny

This is a jewel of an adult movie. In fact, some have hailed this little known picture as one of the all-time best adult films. Constance Money is very attractive, the story is cute, and there is a lot of well-crafted eroticism throughout the picture.

The story is about Ned and Mary, a modern, open-minded couple. Their only problem is with Ned. He is often premature in his coupling habits. Seeking help, they invoke none other than the Prince of Darkness himself, who sends a magical personage called The Arranger. He gives Ned a lotion that helps him maintain an aroused state perpetually. Ned is so proud of himself, he decides to take his sexual aberration to a swinging party. The results are hilarious.

The erotic action in the film is non-stop, often at the sake of the story, but it is so swift and quickly paced that it never bogs down. The jokes are not for the pure of mind, nor are the visuals, which are very explicit.

Of note, there is an excellent underwater sequence between the luscious Constance Money and John Leslie. Elsewhere as well, the production values are superior and professional. Constance and Sharon also have a very arousing scene together in a funky boutique. This is a highly recommended adult film.

Genre: Graphic
Year: 1977
Time: 80 min.
Acting: Very Good
Casting: Good

Script: Good
Production: Good
Directing: Very Good
Theme: Swinging Couples
Humor: Yes

★ Watchable   ★★★ Must See
★★ Recommended   ★★★★ Masterpiece

EDITH MASSEY

Edith Massey was working as a waitress in a sleazy Baltimore pub when underground filmmaker John Waters discovered her. While she is by no means an attractive woman —aging, plump, acute dental deterioration, unpleasant voice—he saw that she had an odd sort of presence. He said that within a few weeks she had transformed the pub from a dreary, dull place into a lively, talkative, friendly environment. It was because of this that he cast her as the "Egg Lady" in Pink Flamingos, and has been a stable actress with him ever since.

Her biggest role was probably the wicked queen of Mortville in Desperate Living. She also stands out in Female Trouble as Divine's obnoxious mother-in-law who is disappointed that her son didn't turn out to be gay.

Edith Massey does have a certain screen presence, but it is difficult to say whether it is an alluring or a repulsive one. She does have character, life, energy, and a certain charm, but Waters's use of the woman is a satirical one. He props her up as the symbol of the perfect woman, much in the same way the typical Playboy Bunny is glorified as the perfect sex symbol. Edith Massey as a joke, however, has probably been over-used.

M

THE MASTERS & MS. JOHNSON ★★

Producer/director: Peter Balakoff
Cast: Larry Moore, Dawn Perry, Halevah, Jennifer West, Vivi Vallin, R.J. Reynolds, William Margold

There is nothing subtle or sophisticated about this film. As a wacky, no-holds-barred, gutter-minded spoof of pop psychology, it is really too silly and strange. But it has some rather strong belly laughs to it, giving it a worthwhile impression.

Drs. Strudelwasser and Johnson run a research center for the sexually disturbed. The patients include an introverted neurotic with a penchant for the one-liner, a psychosomatically blind muscle man (who believes masturbation has done it to him), a jealous lesbian, a couple of transvestites, a flasher, and others. The doctors are assisted by three sex surrogates—two females and one male. The bulk of the story takes place during a "come as you think you are" party.

The eroticism caters to just about every offbeat, nonviolent desire imaginable, and the cast and filmmakers seemed to have had fun making this picture. But unfortunately, the craftsmanship and technical aspects are often lacking.

Genre: Graphic	**Script:** Good
Year: 1981	**Production:** Fair
Time: 79 min.	**Directing:** Fair
Acting: Fair	**Theme:** Hospital Patients
Casting: Fair	**Humor:** Yes

★ Watchable   ★★★ Must See
★★ Recommended   ★★★★ Masterpiece

M

MISBEHAVIN'

Director: Chuck Vincent
Cast: Lesllie Bovèe, Gloria Leonard, Kurt Mann, Dick Gallan,
  Arcadia, Molly Malone

Misbehavin' is a lightly amusing adult film. It has a lot of soft
comedy sprinkled with some titillating erotic encounters, and
some adorable characters.

The story is a takeoff on the story of Job, but there is nothing
religious about it. An angel and a devil make a bet over
whether or not a socialite named Rita, who is getting divorced
for her 13th time, will re-marry for love or money. To hedge
their bets, both the angel and the devil get in on the action,
which turns out to have some wacky overtones.

Both Lesllie Bovèe (as Rita) and Arcadia give outstanding
performances. Their erotic scenes are fun and delightful, bor-
dering on the long side, but interestingly sensual all the same.
The movie does not lack for erotic visuals, and is a feast for
fans of intense and open sexuality.

The technical aspects are fairly good and well within the
watchable spectrum. The show's strong point, however, is in
the affectionate story and characters.

Genre: Graphic
Year: 1979
Time: 84 min.
Acting: Good
Casting: Good

Script: Good
Production: Very Good
Directing: Very Good
Theme: Angels
Humor: Yes

★ Watchable   ★★★ Must See
★★ Recommended   ★★★★ Masterpiece

M

MONDO CANE ★★

Director: Gualtiero Jacopetti
Associate Director: Palo Cavara, Franco Prosperi

This is the first of Jacopetti's famous "shockumentaries," so labeled because of their documentary format. The film contains bona fide cultural antics, but it's real purpose is simply to repulse and humor the audience, not really to document a subject.

Mondo Cane contains about 30 short incidents ranging from a tribute ceremony to Valentino in Southern Italy to naked nubile Trobriand islanders chasing prospective mates, to drunker Germans vomiting in the streets of Hamburg, to cargo cults in New Guinea. One of the most gripping scenes is the "running with the bulls" ceremony in Portugal, where the camera zooms in on young men being gored by wild bulls. Another bloody scene is a ritual in Calabria where young men lacerate their legs with broken glass and run bleeding through the streets on Good Friday celebrating the death of Christ. Then a posh restaurant in New York where people eat fried ants, muskrats, butterflies and other insects is juxtaposed against another restaurant in Hong Kong, where the clients are eating crocodiles, dogs, toads and snakes.

There is nothing sensual or erotic about this movie. The only nudity allowed is among native girls, which is like looking at a National Geographic in the old days before men's magazines. Mondo Cane, although mild by today's standards, was the first film to bring the taboo subjects of violent religious rituals and live-animal slaughter to adult films.

Genre: Taboo	**Script:** Good
Year: 1961	**Production:** Very Good
Time: 105 min.	**Directing:** Very Good
Acting: Good	**Theme:** Native Girls
Casting: Good	**Humor:** Yes

M

MONTENEGRO

Director: Dusan Makavejev
Cast: Susan Anspach, Erland Josephson, Per Oscarsson

A delightful study into the disintegrating psychology of a bored and frustrated housewife. It is funny, very erotic, passionate, and riddled with jabs into society's snobbish attitude toward sexual fulfillment.

A very wealthy American woman is married to a dull Swedish businessman. When the husband is about to leave for Brazil, she decides to go along with him, but is held up in customs and misses the plane. Trying to get back home, she is caught up in the life-style of a group of vibrant Yugoslavian immigrants living in Sweden. She falls in love with the quirky manners of the group and decides to stay for a couple of days, ending up in a romantic affair with one of the workers, singing in a topless bar, and having a lot of fun.

In contrast to Makavejev's other noteworthy films, *WR—Mysteries of the Organism* and *Sweet Movie*, *Montenegro* is light and uncomplicated. It's a simple story simply told. The message is the same—sexual repression leads to insanity, but sensual indulgence livens the spirit.

Montenegro does not exploit its eroticism; it lets it grow out of the situation, out of the characters. When Susan Anspach is seen taking a shower, it is photographed in a very beautiful, soft manner. When a couple is making love, the camera pans up their reeling bodies only long enough to establish their lovemaking, then moves on. All-in-all, this is a top-notch adult film.

Genre: Erotic	**Script:** Very Good
Year: 1981	**Production:** Good
Time: 98 min.	**Directing:** Very Good
Acting: Very Good	**Theme:** Bored Housewife
Casting: Very Good	**Humor:** Yes

MS. MAGNIFICENT ★★

Producer: Damon Christian
Director: Joe Sherman
Cast: Desiree Cousteau, Jesie St. James, Holly McCall, Dan Sir, Larry Davis, John Seeman

This is a comic-book movie, but definitely for adults only. It seems like a film version of the strips one reads in *Penthouse* or *Playboy*. The production was quite elaborate and involves a lot of pop science-fiction sets.

The campy story is basically an erotic version of Superman, though with a lusty woman in the lead. Ms. Magnificent is a protectorate of sexuality, and often helps men find erotic happiness in times of need. When an evil Pirate Queen comes to earth in her spaceship to lock up the planet's sensuality, Ms. Magnificent comes to the rescue.

Much of the film's raw, offbeat humor is hampered by too much time spent on the heroine's sexual bouts, which are prodigious (and explicit). It keeps the film from really flying into orbit. Ms. Magnificent does have a bang-up ending, but the film's charm comes from its amateurish, space-clad cast, who seem to have really enjoyed making this one.

Genre: Graphic
Year: 1979
Time: 84 min.
Acting: Fair
Casting: Fair

Script: Good
Production: Very Good
Directing: Fair
Theme: Super Heroine
Humor: Yes

★ Watchable   ★★★ Must See
★★ Recommended   ★★★★ Masterpiece

N

NAKED CAME THE STRANGER

Director: Henry Paris
Cast: Darby Lloyd Rains, Levi Richards, Mary Stuart

This is a wonderfully appealing light comedy from the maker of *The Opening of Misty Beethoven*. It has some good performances, humor, and some very good editing.

Gillian and William Blake are a married couple who host a radio talk show. After each show, William runs off for a quick afternoon affair with his secretary. One day, Gillian finds out about it and decides to do some fooling around herself. The rest of the film is about the antics of each spouse and their wild daytime activities.

The sensual encounters are mildly comedic with enough realism to make them exciting. Darby is a very fine actress who can put a lot of sexiness in almost anything she does, but without making it raunchy.

The film is filled with one-liners, and has some clever filmmaking techniques, including a silent movie spoof. Henry Paris (Radley Metzger) knows his craft, and his feeling for editing and story pacing is quite good.

Genre: Graphic
Year: 1975
Time: 85 min.
Acting: Very Good
Casting: Good

Script: Good
Production: Good
Directing: Good
Theme: Afternoon Sex
Humor: Yes

NEON NIGHTS ★★★

Producer/director: Cecil Howard
Cast: Lysa Thatcher, Kandi Barbour, Veronica Hart, Arcadia
Lake, Jody Maxwell

A slightly eerie, offbeat film, though not quite weird enough
to be avant-garde.

A young girl named Sandy is forced to leave home after she
is caught romantically entangled in the arms of her mother's
lover. Told that she had a twin sister, she decides it's a good
time to start looking for her. In her search, she comes across a
magician who specializes in levitation, a strange balloon lady,
and an evil socialite who tries to use Sandy for nothing more
than sexual gratification.

The film never really dips into pure exploitation. It does
linger a bit long with some of the more graphic sequences.
The film tries to become more than just a flippant adult movie,
but falls short of escaping the genre. It's a good round of
exotic entertainment, and should have a lot of appeal.

Genre: Graphic
Year: 1982
Time: 90 min.
Acting: Good
Casting: Good

Script: Good
Production: Very Good
Directing: Very Good
Theme: Young Girl
Humor: Yes

★ Watchable ★★★ Must See
★★ Recommended ★★★★ Masterpiece

SUSAN NERO

Susan Nero is originally from Boston, Massachusetts. She moved to the Bay Area in 1978 where she met a young actor in the adult-film business. He claimed that because of her large breasts and sensuous face, she might get a job doing some adult films. She has quickly become a regular in many features, but as of yet has not landed a leading role.

Susan has admitted that she prefers to work with women on the set, but does not pursue this particular fetish in her private life. She has appeared in Pro Ball Cheerleaders, Daisy Mae, Baby Talk, The Wedding, "11," Garage Girls, Centerfold Fever, Fantasy, One Way At a Time, Tropic of Desire, Exposed, For the Love of Pleasure, and Beyond Your Wildest Dreams.

She currently lives in New York where she also works as a figure model and a burlesque dancer.

NEVER SO DEEP

Director: Gerard Damiano
Cast: Loni Sanders, Mike Ranger, Maria Tortuga, Serena, Tara
Aire, Anna Turner

One of Damiano's most recent adult ventures, this film is
among his very best. It's dirty, witty and, of course, sexy.

A successful publisher searches for a hot little hooker he
once encountered in San Francisco's Tenderloin district. The
only thing he remembers about her, other than the fact that
she was terrific, is a little butterfly tattoo on her posterior. He
hires a pretty female investigator to find her, and besides getting into some sexy adventures of her own, the female snoop
has a big problem—almost every girl she comes across has a
butterfly on her derriere.

In keeping with Damiano's style, the sex is flippant, riddled
with bathroom humor, uninhibited, and relentless. But it's
this indulgence that makes Damiano's humor work.

Carol Doda, the famous San Francisco topless dancer/
nightclub owner, has a cameo in the film, and Richard
Pacheco does a wonderful bit as a Pakistani intrigued with the
sexual nature of the famous North Beach district.

Genre: Graphic
Year: 1982
Time: 87 min.
Acting: Good
Casting: Fair

Script: Good
Production: Good
Directing: Good
Theme: Reporter
Humor: Yes

★ Watchable   ★★★ Must See
★★ Recommended   ★★★★ Masterpiece

171

KELLY NICHOLS

Kelly Nichols grew up in California, living primarily in Los Angeles and San Francisco. She first became interested in the modeling world as a make-up artist, and moved to New York to become a photographer's stylist. Her sleek body and good looks were successfully translated on camera. She's been a popular figure model, appearing in Penthouse, Oui, Japanese Playboy, Club, and Chic. Her first film role was with Chuck Vincent in Bon Appetit, where she played the lead.

Kelly has played in such adult fare as Games Women Play, Sex Boat, That Lucky Stiff, Roommates, and Society Affairs. She has also appeared in some R-rated horror films, The Tool Box Murders and It's Murder Baby being two of them.

NIGHTDREAMS ★★★

Director: F. X. Pope
Cast: Dorothy LeMay, Kevin Jay, Andy Nichols, Jennifer West, Danielle, Ken Starbuck

This film is a visual feast. The story is thin, but the photography is so eerie and compelling that the film lingers, dream-like, long afterward.

The "story" concerns the erotic fantasies of a test subject in a sex-therapy clinic. With the use of wires and electronic gadgets, scientists are able to stimulate a woman into unbelievable sensual heights, but they have no way of "seeing" what the subject is dreaming. We, the audience, can see her erotic fantasies in pulsating, living color.

They are vivid, often explicit, and bizarre excursions into dream-time eroticism. We are thrust into the den of a fiery demon where he tortures his victims into erotic frenzy. We visit the smoke-filled tent of a group of Arab sheiks as they maul a writhing woman. We encounter two model-type cowgirls living out a lesbian fantasy, and much more.

The film's visual imagery makes it one of the strangest, most exotic pictures to have ever treated explicit sex. There is no real characterization. The scientists' dialogue is often stilted (even too stilted for scientists) and the ending is badly illogical. The film's positive points, however, greatly outweigh its unpolished moments.

Genre: Graphic
Year: 1981
Time: 78 min.
Acting: Good
Casting: Good

Script: Good
Production: Very Good
Directing: Very Good
Theme: Erotic Dreams
Humor: No

★ Watchable   ★★★ Must See
★★ Recommended   ★★★★ Masterpiece

N

THE NIGHT PORTER   ★★★½

Producers: Robert Gordon Edwards and E. de Simone
Director: Liliana Cavani
Cast: Charlotte Rampling, Dirk Bogarde, Philippe Leroy,
  Gabriele Ferzetti

An unsettling trip into decadence, eroticism, and bondage. It
is excellently photographed and edited. There is much artistry in the acting, especially by Dirk Bogarde, who is able to
genuinely convey strong mixed emotions.

An ex-Nazi scientist hides out as a porter in a German hotel
after the War. One day a very rich woman enters the
establishment, a woman he recognizes as one of his
concentration-camp sex-experiment subjects. She recognizes
him too, but instead of turning him over to the authorities, she
strikes up a dead and perverse relationship with him and slips
back into her role as a sex slave.

The film carefully moves from a slightly romantic dalliance
to a guilt-ridden, sexually perverse relationship between the
two people, ending in a controversial scene where the woman
is chained inside an apartment and repeatedly raped.

Most distrubing is the film's plausibility, despite its rather
unorthodox development.

The film is not necessarily titillating, but seriously portrays
the damage that can be done by sexual abuse.

Genre: Erotic	**Script:** Very Good
Year: 1973	**Production:** Very Good
Time: 115 min.	**Directing:** Good
Acting: Excellent	**Theme:** Bondage
Casting: Very Good	**Humor:** No

NOTHING TO HIDE ★★★

Director: Anthony Spinelli
Cast: John Leslie, Richard Pacheco, Elizabeth Randolph,
Chelsea Manchester, Raven Turner, Misty Ragen

This bold adult film tries to portray real, everyday people who also happen to be highly sexed. The story is strong, with two very likable characters.

The film is billed as the sequel to *Talk Dirty To Me*. It continues the adventures of a fast-talking playboy named Jack and his bungling sidekick, Lenny. Whereas the first film concentrated on Jack, this one focuses on Lenny. He wants a woman, and talks Jack into having one of his girlfriends sleep with him, but when she makes fun of him, he runs away. In a nearby park, he bumps into an equally pathetic girl. After a brief courtship, Lenny decides to get married, even though Jack advises against it.

The treatment of sex is realistic. It is not the usual flippant, joke-ridden stuff, which may be good or bad, depending on what one wants in a film. For those who think of eroticism as serious, it will be appealing, especially as the two adorable misfits, Lenny and his girlfriend, attempt to make love.

As an actor, Richard Pacheco (Lenny) really shines, showing that he has a deft talent for strong, attractive characters.

Overall, however, the movie tries a little too hard and becomes too sentimental near the end. It would have been better to concentrate on its lighter, more humorous moments.

Genre: Graphic
Year: 1981
Time: 101 min.
Acting: Very Good
Casting: Good

Script: Good
Production: Good
Directing: Very Good
Theme: Picking Up Girls
Humor: Yes

★ Watchable ★★★ Must See
★★ Recommended ★★★★ Masterpiece

O

OCTOBER SILK ★★

Director: Henri Pachard
Cast: Abigail Clayton, Candida Royalle, Lisa DeLeeuw,
Gloria Leonard

Henri Pachard has refined the vignette-type film almost to an
art form. But this effort—despite some worthy erotic performances and wall-to-wall sex—falls victim to its format.

The "story" spins off a high-fashion boutique called
Gloria's whose customers are mainly interested in items for
their nocturnal erotic exploits. The film simply follows these
crazed pursuers of sensual delights through their adventures.

The eroticism caters to almost every adult situation imaginable. Of note are a scene in which a lady in traction is constantly teased by a cute nurse, and another in which Gloria
Leonard "helps" a couple of virgins.

October Silk has had enormous success as an adult film. For
the fans of the genre, its slight story and abundance of lusty
adventure is quite appealing. To a broader audience, however,
the film may be too slow.

Genre: Graphic
Year: 1980
Time: 80 min.
Acting: Good
Casting: Good

Script: Fair
Production: Very Good
Directing: Good
Theme: Sales Girls
Humor: Yes

ODYSSEY ★★★

Director: Gerard Damiano
Cast: Susan McBain, C.J. Laing, Vanessa Del Rio

Gerard Damiano takes a tough premise and wrings top-notch performances out of his cast. A superior film.

A series of vignettes explores many of the sexual hang-ups, frustrations, guilt feelings, and taboos in society. Each episode takes up one of these problems: homosexuality, clothes fetishes, alternate orifice indulgences, whips and chains, and other exotic, forbidden pleasures.

Damiano takes great care in photographing and pacing each erotic scene into a powerful climax. Although the story is quite weak, it is the sort of movie one can begin watching in the middle without worrying about continuity. In fact, the film is so potent that it might be better to catch it little by little.

Genre: Graphic
Year: 1979
Time: 90 min.
Acting: Very Good
Casting: Excellent

Script: Poor
Production: Good
Directing: Very Good
Theme: Sex Hang-Ups
Humor: Yes

★ Watchable ★★★ Must See
★★ Recommended ★★★★ Masterpiece

O

THE OPENING OF MISTY BEETHOVEN ★★★★

Producer/director: Henry Paris
Cast: Constance Money, Jamie Gillis, Jacqueline Beaudant, Gloria Leonard

An erotic classic, a jewel. The story is swift, the cast good-looking, especially Constance Money, and the performances energetic, erotic, and quite excellent. The cinematography is sophisticated for a low-budget film and the plot affords movement from one intensely erotic scene to another, building to an all-out climax.

The premise evokes *My Fair Lady*. Seymour Love is a member of the ultra-high class whose hobby is sex writing. While researching in Paris, he finds a common street hooker whom he thinks can be transformed into a top-flight prostitute. Another member of the jet set doesn't agree, and they make a wager.

Nothing is left to the imagination. The sex is graphic, energetic, and fun to watch. There is a slight tongue-in-cheek approach that makes it both erotic and delightful. Misty is taught how to handle other women, two or three men at a time, various positions, and a variety of sex aids. There is something for everyone.

Constance Money is adorable. She plays a demanding yet simple role with a lot of nerve and talent, especially for eroticism, and is totally convincing.

Other roles are equally well-cast, especially the sensitive yet firm mentor played by Jamie Gillis. This film is indeed a sublime piece of erotic art. Many consider it to be the best all-around adult film ever made.

Genre: Graphic
Year: 1976
Time: 88 min.
Acting: Very Good
Casting: Very Good

Script: Very Good
Production: Excellent
Directing: Very Good
Theme: Prostitute
Humor: Yes

THE OTHER SIDE OF JULIE ★★

Director: Anthony Riverton
Cast: Susannah French, John Leslie, Jackie O'Neill, Paula Donnely, Joe Maseria, Kristine Heller

This film stands apart from the pack of adult films for a number of reasons. It has an interesting story, a leading lady who's portrayed as a real person—instead of just a sex object—high production values, and good, frequent erotic encounters.

The story concerns a struggling middle-class American couple, or so we think. The husband is actually a gigolo trading sexual favors for money. One day, his wife walks in on him "working," and out of spite and curiosity, she embarks on her own orgiastic odyssey.

Sexuality is treated with absolute frankness and explicitness, but often dips into cliche and flat humor. Nevertheless, the wife comes across as a believable, sexually strong woman who's ultra-aggressive.

Unfortunately, few of these performers can act. Susannah French tries very hard, and just barely pulls it off.

Genre: Graphic
Year: 1978
Time: 90 min.
Acting: Good
Casting: Good

Script: Very Good
Production: Good
Directing: Good
Theme: Cheating Housewife
Humor: No

★ Watchable ★★★ Must See
★★ Recommended ★★★★ Masterpiece

O

OUTLAW LADIES ★★★

Director: Henri Pachard
Cast: Marlene Willoughby, Jody Maxwell, Juliet Anderson,
Samantha Fox, Veronica Hart

Like *October Silk* and *Babylon Pink,* this is a vignette film
with a very loose storyline. The production values are high,
the acting erotic and the overall effect quite stimulating. It's
director Pachard's best episodic film.

Five wealthy and society-conscious ladies have very strong
sex drives but are concerned about their reputation. To fulfill
their hidden vices and remain anonymous, they devise elaborate games, which lead to some very comic situations. For
example, two of the ladies pick up some joker at a sleazy bar
and end up having a threesome in his flop-joint apartment.
Another woman runs an "escort" service on the side, sometimes using her own mansion when her husband is gone.

The sex is treated with affection, mystery, and lust. The
actresses always thoroughly enjoy what they are doing, especially Marlene Willoughby, who always seems to have her
tongue implanted firmly in cheek.

By nature the film caters to fans who like to see a lot of sex,
but the director spends some time with the antics of the
ladies' business careers as well. Pachard shows the irony of
women being treated as sex objects in the business world, yet
being the sexual aggressors in private life.

It's a fun film. Hustler magazine rated it Number One in
1981.

Genre: Graphic	**Script:** Fair
Year: 1981	**Production:** Good
Time: 83 min.	**Directing:** Very Good
Acting: Very Good	**Theme:** Bored Housewives
Casting: Good	**Humor:** Yes

P—TALK ★★

Director: Frederic Lanzac
Cast: Penelope Lamour, Sylvia Bourdon, Ellen Earl-Coupey

The French answer to *Deep Throat*. Instead of a clitoris in the throat, Joan discovers that she has her vocal cords somewhere else. Her regular voice is soft and sweet, but the second one is raspy, sexy, and uninhibited—which gets her into a number of hilarious situations.

Though the film has the glossy, high-production standards typical of French erotic cinema, the characters are somewhat flat and the sex scenes are often forced. Nevertheless, it succeeds quite well as a sex comedy. For instance, after the voice gets her involved in a group scene in a restroom, it starts relating some of Joan's more infamous sexual exploits, much to the shy woman's dismay.

The sex scenes are frequent and graphic and are filled with stylized humor.

Genre: Erotic	**Script:** Fair
Year: 1975	**Production:** Very Good
Time: 91 min.	**Directing:** Good
Acting: Good	**Theme:** Housewife
Casting: Good	**Humor:** Yes

★	Watchable	★★★	Must See
★★	Recommended	★★★★	Masterpiece

P

PANDORA'S MIRROR ★★½

Director: Warren Evans
Cast: Veronica Hart, Sandra Hillman, Jamie Gillis, George
   Payne, Tiffany Clark

This movie contains some nice production values, good cos-
tumes, and above-average performances for an adult film. The
erotic situations are also well done.

It is about a magic mirror that is a portal into the past.
Pandora, while window shopping with her friend, comes
across it. She takes it home, and while staring into its reflec-
tion, finds herself living out erotic fantasies that take place in
the past.

While the film is deliberately slow-paced, the sexual encounters are intense. Veronica Hart and Tiffany Clark have
outstanding scenes, especially the scene where Veronica is
being mauled by a gang of lascivious young men. The erotic
scenes are tender and soft on the whole, however.

The film is solid entertainment with some very polished
cinematography and sets. It caters to audiences of both sexes.

Genre: Graphic   **Script:** Good
Year: 1981   **Production:** Very Good
Time: 93 min.   **Directing:** Good
Acting: Very Good   **Theme:** Antique Store
Casting: Good   **Humor:** Not Really

★ Watchable   ★★★ Must See
★★ Recommended   ★★★★ Masterpiece

KAY PARKER

Kay Parker is probably one of the most voluptuous older women in adult films. She is well-proportioned, has attractive dark eyes, ivory white skin, and a husky, British accent.

Ms. Parker is usually cast in the part of older women — mothers, step-mothers, rich aunts — but says that her next film, Body Talk, is more in keeping with her true identity.

Kay was born and raised in England. She moved to the United States pursuing a successful career in the import business. While living in San Francisco, she became interested in acting. She studied drama and became involved with an adult-film actor, although she didn't know it at the time. He arranged for her role in V—The Hot One, but it was a nonsexual role. She later met Anthony Spinelli, who cast her in the classic Sex World as a sexually unfulfilled housewife. After that, she did a number of adult films, including Chorus Call, Seven Into Snowy, and Untamed. She eventually quit the import business and moved to Los Angeles, pursuing a career in film. She has since done Downstairs/Upstairs, The Health Spa, Kate and the Indians, The Dancers and her notorious Taboo, where she plays the incestuous mother.

Outside the adult-film business, Kay has been getting small parts on television and in some big Hollywood movies. Recently, she played a cameo in the opening sequence of The Best Little Whorehouse in Texas.

P

PINK CHAMPAGNE ★★

Director: Steven Conrad
Cast: John Steele, Lisa DeLeeuw, Rick Fonte, Aimee Leigh, Jeff Parker

A comedy with elaborate sets, this feature seems to say, "Do it big, with or without polish."

The film is a takeoff on Hollywood's perennial Great Talent Hunts. In this case, a big-time Hollywood producer and his wife are auditioning young ladies to find tomorrow's superstars. In reality, he is just lining up a bunch of naive, pretty young girls for some lusty pleasures.

The film affords a lot of room to dwell on the erotic encounters, which are abundant. To keep them from becoming tedious, the film often interjects humor into the sequences, occasionally hitting the mark.

Lisa DeLeeuw, playing the wife of the producer, is particularly fiesty. She, too, must "try out" the auditioning young ladies. All in all, *Pink Champagne* is a lot of fun.

Genre: Graphic	**Script:** Fair
Year: 1980	**Production:** Good
Time: 76 min.	**Directing:** Fair
Acting: Fair	**Theme:** Casting Couch
Casting: Good	**Humor:** Yes

PINK FLAMINGOS ★

Producer/director/writer: John Waters
Cast: Divine, David Lochary, Mink Stole, Mary Vivian Pearcy,
Edith Massey, Danny Mills

Giving this film any sort of rating would be a travesty. By
intent, it is a non-movie, a negative film that caters to the dark
side of human nature. It is unrealistic, over-indulgent and
sick. Its ultra-low budget, cast without acting ability, and uninspired cinematography add to its repulsion. And yet, *Pink
Flamingos* claims a strong and loyal cult following, still
playing in the midnight slot in many art theaters around the
country. For that, we give it a single star; for the rest it actually
deserves a negative rating. It is precisely this negativeness,
this black humor, that makes the film work. One can't help
chuckling from time to time at this strange and volcanic
movie.

The story revolves around a feud between the lead character, Divine, and the Marbles, as they vie for the title of being
the "filthiest people in the world." Like a one-on-one sporting
event, the two sides try to out-gross each other. Some of their
filthy deeds include mailing human feces, kidnapping female
hitchhikers, impregnating them, and selling the babies to lesbian couples, spreading saliva over the opponent's furniture,
incest, castration, cannibalism, torture, rape, and murder.

There is certainly nothing erotic in this movie, and all use
of sex, explicitly and otherwise, is for shock value and not
sensuality.

Genre: Taboo
Year: 1973
Time: 95 min.
Acting: Fair
Casting: Very Good

Script: Fair
Production: Poor
Directing: Very Good
Theme: Transvestism
Humor: Yes

★	Watchable	★★★	Must See
★★	Recommended	★★★★	Masterpiece

P

THE PINK LADIES ★★

Director: Richard Mahler
Cast: Vanessa Del Rio, Samantha Fox, Kandi Barbour, Robin Byrd, Marlene Willoughby, Christine de Shaffer

A fairly standard adult film with some interesting variations on a theme, some potent images, and a bunch of very aggressive, dominant, and devious women.

Four bored housewives try to brighten up their sex lives with games and fantasies. While this is probably the most common plot in adult films, the movie still has some clever twists. The sexually adventurous women often meet their husbands without knowing them and engage in erotic interludes. Other times, wives switch husbands—and, during the fantasy sequences, all logic flies out the window.

The husbands' fantasy about Vanessa Del Rio is particularly lusty. It is indulgent and explicit, as most of the other encounters are. While the story is standard, it is developed and detailed much more cleverly than the average adult film. Best of all, it's a pleasant, stimulating excursion into both male and female erotic fantasies.

Genre: Graphic	**Script:** Fair
Year: 1980	**Production:** Very Good
Time: 80 min.	**Directing:** Good
Acting: Good	**Theme:** Bored Housewife
Casting: Good	**Humor:** Yes

PLATINUM PARADISE ★★★

Director: Cecil Howard
Cast: Samantha Fox, Bobby Astyr, Hillary Summers, Kandi Barbour, Christie Ford, Eric Edwards

While this is another vignette-style film, it has some very clever aspects to it. The photography and music are very effective and almost all the performers are enthusiastic and zesty without becoming overbearing. It's a very attractive movie.

Platinum Paradise is about an answering service run by an extremely mischievous operator who gets her kicks out of crossing lines, giving unasked wake-up calls in the middle of the night, and letting the "wrong" person overhear a very intimate phone conversation.

Using the answering service as a springboard, we jump into the sex lives of many of the customers. There is a soft and sensitive deflowering scene, and a frenzied lesbian encounter, as well as other standard adult situations.

The movie is rhythmic, almost dreamlike in construction and is remarkably swift-paced for an adult film. It affords a lot of intense erotic screen time with little loss of interest.

Genre: Graphic
Year: 1980
Time: 80 min.
Acting: Fair
Casting: Good

Script: Good
Production: Good
Directing: Good
Theme: Secretary
Humor: Yes

★ Watchable	★★★ Must See
★★ Recommended	★★★★ Masterpiece

P

PLATO'S, THE MOVIE

Director: Joe Sherman
Cast: Seka, Lisa DeLeeuw, Mike Ranger, William Margold, Rebecca Savage

This movie really tried to be a good one, but somewhere something went wrong. Although it has some better-than-average cinematography, the acting is fair to poor and the story is kind of dumb. In the end, however, this movie is so convoluted and silly that it actually becomes entertaining.

The setting is the now defunct Plato's Retreat—once a notorious, uninhibited swinger's club in California. A man mysteriously dies in the club because of his intense sexual activity and a newspaper editor puts his two best reporters on the job. Those two reporters are great-looking women with ample bustlines and a penchant for erotic situations. Thus, Seka and Lisa end up undercover (read uncovered) in the sex club and have some pretty bizarre adventures.

The club sex scenes are big, orgiastic, and thoroughly indulgent. The "fantasy room," where partners are separated by a big plastic curtain with a mouth-sized hole in it is a very arousing device. But too many of the other erotic scenes tend to be long and uneventful.

On the whole, the movie's plot has so many turns and twists that it takes almost five minutes of a volcanic verbal eruption at the end to unravel it. It would have been better to have done it visually. *Plato's* has some appealing eroticism, but is really not much of a film.

Genre: Graphic	**Script:** Fair
Year: 1980	**Production:** Good
Time: 80 min.	**Directing:** Fair
Acting: Poor	**Theme:** Swinging Couples
Casting: Fair	**Humor:** Yes

PLEASE MR. POSTMAN   ★

Director: Louis Lewis
Cast: Loni Sanders, Nicole Noir, Paul Thomas

This movie is basically a showcase for the sensual appetites of Loni Sanders, one of the prettiest actresses in the adult-film business. She can't make up for the film's other deficiencies, however.

A lady letter carrier in a small town gets involved in one erotic tangle after another as she delivers the mail. To one man, she hands over a blow-up sex doll, to another a nightgown, to another a box full of sex toys. She always sticks around while the person opens the package, which is how she keeps getting involved.

The sex is illogical and wrought with standard adult formulas, but manages to be a turn-on anyway.

Genre: Graphic
Year: 1981
Time: 72 min.
Acting: Fair
Casting: Poor

Script: Fair
Production: Good
Directing: Fair
Theme: Postwoman
Humor: Yes

★ Watchable   ★★★ Must See
★★ Recommended   ★★★★ Masterpiece

P

PORTRAIT OF SEDUCTION

Director: Anthony Spinelli
Cast: Vicky Lyon, Robert Cole, Jeffrey Stern, Monique Cardin,
Rita Stone

In its portrayal of raw lust, this film gets high marks, but the
technical aspects are uneven and some of the performers can't
act.

Three months after a couple are married, the man's artistic
son moves in with them. The woman's stepson seduces her
and she confesses the affair to her mother (all told in
flashback).

The sex is realistic, almost shocking. There is a lot of "back
door" action and some quasi-rape sequences that become
passionate embraces. In one mild bondage scene, the young
man forces his stepmother into a lesbian liaison.

The film occasionally borders on the brutal. Vicky Lyon
does a fair job as the mature stepmother and she is terrific in
her seduction scenes.

Genre: Graphic   **Script:** Fair
Year: 1976   **Production:** Good
Time: 76 min.   **Directing:** Good
Acting: Good   **Theme:** Seduction
Casting: Good   **Humor:** No

PRETTY PEACHES ★★★

Director: Alex DeRenzy
Cast: Desiree Cousteau, John Leslie, Joey Civera, Eileen Welles, Nancy Hoffman, Sharon Kane

This is a fun picture. The acting isn't great, the cinematography is only adequate, but the plot is well done for an adult movie and there are some good comic situations.

A pretty but dumb young lady gets in a car accident, then suffers amnesia. Two clever young men find her and claim her car is theirs. Thinking that she might be rich, they decide to help her find her past, and the film chronicles the dizzy girl's hilarious misadventures.

The sexual encounters are often bizarre, potent with sensuality, and contain exotic fetishes. Alex DeRenzy shines in his offbeat eroticism, and this film is a good example of his quasi-erotic, bathroom humor.

Desiree Cousteau won an erotica award for her performance, and whether or not one calls it acting, she has charm and charisma and is delightful to watch.

Genre: Graphic
Year: 1978
Time: 82 min.
Acting: Good
Casting: Fair

Script: Good
Production: Good
Directing: Good
Theme: Young Girl
Humor: Yes

★ Watchable ★★★ Must See
★★ Recommended ★★★★ Masterpiece

P

PRISONER OF PARADISE ★★

Directors: Gail Palmer and Bob Chinn
Cast: John Holmes, Seka, Sue Carol, Nikki Anderson,
Heinz Mueller

Some remarkably high-budget footage can be found here, but the film is pretty brutal. The performers, despite only fair acting jobs, shine in the intense, erotic sequences.

A shipwrecked sailor (John Holmes) is washed up on a desert island. Thinking he is alone, he reflects back to the good times in Hawaii, especially with his Oriental girlfriend. But he soon discovers that the island isn't uninhabited—there is a camp of Nazis who have captured and are torturing two American nurses. The sailor jumps to the rescue, but gets caught himself.

The sex is filled with sadistic overtones, torture, and pain, but for the kind of movie it is, the treatment is restrained. The film contains a number of intensely erotic rape scenes, including some lesbian seductions.

Seka is okay as an evil Nazi SS officer, especially as she "interrogates" one of the nurses. The film has been highly regarded by many adult film critics.

Genre: Graphic
Year: 1980
Time: 82 min.
Acting: Fair
Casting: Good

Script: Good
Production: Very Good
Directing: Good
Theme: Rape
Humor: No

THE PRIVATE AFTERNOONS OF
PAMELA MANN   ★★★

Director: Henry Paris
Cast: Barbara Bourbon, Sonny Landham, Darby Lloyd Rains,
  Jamie Gillis, Marc Stevens, Eric Edwards

A good story and some excellent comic and erotic situations
have made this film something of a classic.

A wealthy businessman who thinks his wife is cheating on
him hires a detective to keep an eye on her, and finds that
she's having an affair with another private detective. The wife
discovers the detective is watching her, so she attempts to
seduce him, and the story weaves deeper and deeper into an
erotic tangle.

The sex is explicit, with Barbara Bourbon demonstrating
her "sword-swallowing" technique. Other scenes include a
kidnapping by two crazed terrorists, some girl-on-girl encounters, and an all-out group sex scene near the end.

The film was one of the first adult productions to attempt
elaborate storytelling by a previously non-adult filmmaker,
Henry Paris. The actors try hard but come off amateurish,
which is unfortunate because *Private Afternoons* has a lot of
potentially funny situations. As adult films go, however, this
one's excellent.

Genre: Graphic	**Script:** Good
Year: 1974	**Production:** Very Good
Time: 83 min.	**Directing:** Very Good
Acting: Good	**Theme:** Housewife
Casting: Good	**Humor:** Yes

★	Watchable	★★★	Must See
★★	Recommended	★★★★	Masterpiece

R

RANDY, THE ELECTRIC LADY ★★★

Director: Philip Schuman
Cast: Desiree Cousteau, Monica Sands, Juliet Anderson,
Roger Frazer

A delightful, creative science fiction spoof. The girls are cute and fun to watch, especially the scatterbrained Desiree Cousteau.

A group of young ladies enters a sex-research center because they cannot achieve orgasm. The center, however, is just a front for a mad female scientist. During one experiment, Randy (Desiree Cousteau) short-circuits the machinery and somehow turns into a human aphrodisiac—anyone she couples with is sent into an erotic orbit.

The sex is very lighthearted, with a lot of teasing building to more explicit bouts.

This is Philip Schuman's first and only venture into adult filmmaking, and he does a great job. Some of the sequences are so cleverly edited that an erotic tension is built with very little happening in the scenes. The girls' training in the gym, for example, is particularly nice and the speeded-up footage of old stag loops is hilarious.

The last third, however, seems to drop in quality, as if the production was running out of money and they rushed to get it finished on a declining budget. All in all, however, the film is a very witty erotic comedy.

Genre: Graphic	**Script:** Good
Year: 1980	**Production:** Good
Time: 84 min.	**Directing:** Very Good
Acting: Fair	**Theme:** Sex Therapy
Casting: Good	**Humor:** Yes

★ Watchable ★★★ Must See
★★ Recommended ★★★★ Masterpiece

Mike Ranger journeyed to Los Angeles from Colorado to get into adult movies. He walked unannounced into the Sunset Agency, then being run by the notorious William Margold. He had such a fresh face and muscular body that Margold quickly cast him in adult films. Ranger has since become a stable in the industry.

He has probably been vastly underrated as an actor. His incredible erotic performances probably hide his other abilities. He has starred in Aunt Peg; Bad Girls; Nanci Blue; Plato's, The Movie; Same Time Every Year; Star Virgin; Sweet Cheeks; Anytime, Anyplace. His most noted film is Taboo, where he plays an incestuous teenager. In the role, he is slightly older-looking than he should be, but his sensual performance is excellent.

Mike Ranger has quit the adult-film business and moved to a rural farm in Washington, where he lives with the sensual star of adult films, Loni Sanders. Loni, however, continues to do an occasional film.

R

HARRY REEMS

Mr. Reems entered the New York theater community in the mid-sixties. He has been a member of such ensembles as Cafe La Mama, The National Shakespeare Company, New York Theatre Ensemble, and Ensemble Studio Theatre. It was during this theater period that Mr. Reems first began doing erotic underground films. He appeared in hundreds of short films before his notable Deep Throat role, which catapulted his name before a large audience.

After Deep Throat, Reems did six or seven films and then retired from the adult film industry. Like Marilyn Chambers, he went on to do more mainstream comedies. It was during this period that his famous trial began. He was indicted by the Federal Government for conspiracy to transport obscene material across a state border. He was convicted in Memphis, Tennessee on April 29, 1976. The conviction was reversed on March 25, 1977.

During the trial, Mr. Reems went on a college-campus lecture tour. After a lecture at Harvard, the president of the Harvard Law School Forum wrote to Reems, "To be honest, you were not at all what we had been expecting, and we were pleasantly surprised not only at your general articulateness, but especially at your knowledge of the legal issues involved in your case and their ramifications."

A similar letter from Tufts University (Massachusetts) said, "Considering the speakers we have had this year—Pat Moynihan, Ralph Nader, Margaret Mead, F. Lee Bailey—one would think that whoever followed them would, comparatively, draw only an average ovation. Not so with your lecture. With a good admixture of humor and education, and being not at all condescending, yours was one of the better talks we've had all year."

His most notable films include Deep Throat, The Devil In Miss Jones, Sometimes Sweet Susan, Wet Rainbow, and Butterflies.

RENDEZVOUS WITH ANNE ★★

Director: Lowell Pickett
Cast: Keri Carpenter, Lisa Troy, Cazander Zim

Though made in the early days of the adult industry, this minor classic contains some surprisingly mature themes, especially in its depiction of explicit sex in an inoffensive, unindulgent manner.

Three young girls at the San Francisco airport mistakenly answer a P.A.-system page that turns out to be for someone else. The girls, all named Anne, make friends and, since all are in the fabled city for vacations, they agree to get together in a couple of weeks to tell about their adventures.

One girl is visiting her boyfriend, and their relationship has been up and down for some time. Another meets a stereotypical San Franciscan artist. The third discovers that her husband has been fooling around, and decides to do some uninhibited erotic pursuing on her own, ending up in an all-out orgy where she finds true happiness.

The sex is played on its erotic merits and not on its shock value. There are no lingering closeups, and "mutual climax" scenes are portrayed very naturally.

Genre: Graphic	**Script:** Good
Year: 1973	**Production:** Fair
Time: 70 min.	**Directing:** Fair
Acting: Poor	**Theme:** Young Girls
Casting: Good	**Humor:** No

★ Watchable   ★★★ Must See
★★ Recommended   ★★★★ Masterpiece

R

THE RESURRECTION OF EVE ★★★

Director: Jim and Artie Mitchell
Cast: Marilyn Chambers, Matthew Armon, Mimi Morgan

A follow-up to Marilyn Chambers's popular debut into adult cinema, this film is in keeping with the Mitchell Brothers previous efforts at attempting serious portrayals of eroticism.

A woman named Eve Goodman has a terrible car accident, undergoes plastic surgery, and emerges a beautiful woman. (Eve is played before the accident by Mimi Morgan and after by Marilyn Chambers.)

Wanting to show off his beautiful wife, the husband drags her reluctantly to a swingers' party. At first she is afraid and bashful, but soon her reservations turn into outright passions, and she becomes the toast of the orgy.

The erotic sequences, as in *Behind the Green Door*, tend to be long but carefully constructed. Miss Chambers, unfortunately, is not the industry's best actress, but her other talents are on ample display here.

Genre: Graphic
Year: 1973
Time: 82 min.
Acting: Fair
Casting: Good

Script: Fair
Production: Good
Directing: Good
Theme: Swinging
Humor: No

THE ROCKY HORROR PICTURE SHOW ★★★

Director: Jim Sharman
Cast: Tim Curry, Susan Sarandon, Barry Bostwick

A gem of a musical that started as a smash play in London, bombed in its initial film release, then scored a phenomenal success on the midnight "cult movie" circuit. Its fanatical following is as unusual as the movie.

A middle-class young couple, motoring in the country on their wedding night, have car trouble in front of a huge mansion. Wanting to use the phone, the two approach the house and go in just as its master, Dr. Frank N. Furter, is conducting an experiment. His newly made creature, the body-beautiful Rocky, is ready to be unveiled, and the innocent couple is caught up in this strange household filled with the doctor's campy, exotically dressed admirers. Both the wife and the husband are seduced by this garter-belted "scientist."

The film's first half is fast and funny, with virtually every song a memorable one. But the second half tries to do too much and the film loses much of its potency. Nevertheless, the offbeat comedy and adorable characters make this a delightful treat.

Genre: Erotic
Year: 1975
Time: 100 min.
Acting: Very Good
Casting: Excellent

Script: Very Good
Production: Excellent
Directing: Very Good
Theme: Transvestism
Humor: Definitely

★ Watchable ★★★ Must See
★★ Recommended ★★★★ Masterpiece

R

ROOMMATES ★★★

Director: Chuck Vincent
Cast: Samantha Fox, Veronica Hart, Kelly Nichols

This serious film attempts to combine graphic sex with drama. While the combination has some problems, the film has a lot of merit and has received much critical acclaim.

The story is simply the day-to-day activities of three New York women sharing an apartment. One is an ex-call girl trying to make it in the advertising industry. Another is a California model experimenting with an offbeat sex life-style in the big city. The third is an actress trying to make it on Broadway.

The action centers on each woman's dealings with the male of the species and how each is mistreated. The actress has an affair with her acting coach, but he drops her for renewed hopes with his wife. The model is abused and constantly beaten by her weird boyfriend. The advertising career woman suffers sexual harassment.

The sex is surprisingly infrequent when compared to most adult movies, but it is both graphic and well-crafted. The major failing of the film is in the drama, which tends to be flat. It is, however, a monumental effort by a traditionally adult filmmaker to create genuine drama within a strong sexual plot.

Genre: Graphic
Year: 1982
Time: 89 min.
Acting: Good
Casting: Good

Script: Good
Production: Very Good
Directing: Very Good
Theme: Models
Humor: No

★ Watchable   ★★★ Must See
★★ Recommended   ★★★★ Masterpiece

CANDIDA ROYALLE

Candida graduated at the top of her high school class and delivered the valedictorian speech at her graduation. She went on to higher education, became a commercial artist, and took on the progressive social attitudes found in her young, budding artistic crowd. After appearing in a few nude skits, she tried out for some more professional sex comedies and discovered that she enjoyed erotic exhibitionism.

She has been featured in a number of adult films, including All The Senator's Girls, Ball Game, Champagne For Breakfast, Delicious, Fascination, Hot Rackets, Hot and Saucy Pizza Girls, That Lucky Stiff, The Tiffany Minx, Ultra Flesh, and recently wrote the feature film Blue Magic, in which she plays the lead.

Candida is still very active in adult films and seems to be getting more involved with behind-the-camera activities.

S

SADIE ★

Director: Bob Chinn
Cast: Chris Cassidy, Jerome Deeds, Diahana Holt

Good production values, good lighting, and photography serve only to make the poor acting and story-line more painfully obvious here.

It is a takeoff of W. Somerset Maugham's classic short story "Rain." This version concentrates on a blonde hooker tossed out of Vietnam during the war. Her crime, of course, is prostitution, and she ends up on a South Sea island with a puritanical senator who continuously preaches morality and virtue to her.

The sensual treatment runs the gamut of adult-film formulas, including lesbianism, groups, and a number of variations on the classic act.

Chris Cassidy, playing the title role, is very appealing and brings a bright, warm spot to the movie.

Genre: Graphic	**Script:** Poor
Year: 1980	**Production:** Very Good
Time: 92 min.	**Directing:** Good
Acting: Poor	**Theme:** Tropical
Casting: Good	**Humor:** No

★ Watchable ★★★ Must See
★★ Recommended ★★★★ Masterpiece

JESIE ST. JAMES

This young lady from San Francisco burst upon the adult movie screen in the sensational Easy, which established her both as a competent actress and a very sexy lady. She is a sleek, classic blonde.

The director of Easy, Anthony Spinelli, said that when he first saw Jesie he fell in love with her. At the time, he had just lost the leading actress, and was desperately looking for a replacement. Once Jesie appeared, he quit looking, and began shooting.

She has appeared in Blonde Fire, Blondes Have More Fun, Fantasy World, Hot Legs, Insatiable, Ms. Magnificent, Talk Dirty To Me, Tropic of Desire, and Indecent Exposure.

S

SALO, 120 DAYS OF SODOM ★★

Director: Pier Paolo Pasolini
Cast: Paolo Bonacelli, Giorgio Cataldi, Uberto P. Quintavalle

Based loosely on the Marquis de Sade's *120 Days of Sodom*, this extremely repulsive film is well made and well acted and tries to delve into the workings of the sick, sadistic mind.

During World War II in Italy, a group of prominent Fascist men and some whores select 18 young political prisoners, evenly divided between women and men, and take them up to a secluded mansion where they are abused sexually and physically.

The abuse, at first, is light. The prisoners, for example, are to accommodate coitus with any of the masters upon request, but as the story unfolds the captives are refused bathroom facilities, forced to engage in coprophagy and later tortured to death.

The film is not for the weak of heart. While it doesn't spend a lot of screen time on the sexual perversions or the gore, it is so realistic that the viewer feels transported into the sadistic household, becoming a sort of accomplice to the atrocities.

Genre: Taboo	**Script:** Good
Year: 1977	**Production:** Good
Time: 117 min.	**Directing:** Very Good
Acting: Good	**Theme:** Torture
Casting: Very Good	**Humor:** No

SAME TIME EVERY YEAR ★★

Director: F. J. Lincoln
Cast: Loni Sanders, Mike Ranger, Tiffany Clark, Jean Damage

Same old plot line—husbands cheating on their wives—but nicely done here with good performances by some very sensual people.

Three men tell their wives they're going to their annual convention, which actually is their annual fling with other women. One husband visits his mistress, another takes on two girls simultaneously, and the third strikes up a liaison with a stripper. Meanwhile, with the husbands away, the wives can play too.

The film is wall-to-wall erotic action, which can tire a movie out, not to mention the actors. The sensual scenes are involving and quite exciting.

Genre: Graphic	**Script:** Fair
Year: 1981	**Production:** Fair
Time: 81 min.	**Directing:** Fair
Acting: Good	**Theme:** Extramarital Affairs
Casting: Good	**Humor:** No

★ Watchable ★★★ Must See
★★ Recommended ★★★★ Masterpiece

S

SATIN SUITE ★★½

Director: Philip Drexler, Jr.
Cast: Samantha Fox, Heather Young, Eric Edwards

Drexler is a director noted for his superior production values, and this one is an early attempt that lives up to many of his later works. It's carefully developed and has nice performances and some very pretty women.

An ultra-aggressive career woman on a high-fashion woman's magazine forfeits her chastity, blackmails her superiors, and engages in other unscrupulous dealing as she claws her way to the top.

The sex situations grow out of the plot—as when the woman gets Eric Edwards into bed while a hidden camera films them. Another sequence follows a car through a car wash as a lively, erotic couple fondle each other inside the vehicle.

The only major flaw is that the story becomes tedious near the end, but otherwise it is a lush excursion into the erotic dealings of a forceful woman.

Genre: Graphic
Year: 1979
Time: 80 min.
Acting: Good
Casting: Good

Script: Fair
Production: Very Good
Directing: Very Good
Theme: Aggressive Woman
Humor: No

THE SATISFIERS OF ALPHA BLUE ★★

Director: Gerard Damiano
Cast: Lysa Thatcher, Richard Bolla, Herschel Savage,
Hillary Summers

An interesting experiment for the prolific Damiano, who has made a lot of significant adult films. In this one he has attempted to combine a strong story with a tremendous amount of sex, and falls just short of scoring a very good movie.

It takes place in a future society where the procreative aspect of sex has been eradicated, including marriage. In fact, most of the everyday aspects of human existence have been swept away, leaving very little for people to do except engage in erotic play.

As in most of these Brave New World scenarios, there is one deadbeat who doesn't like the good life. He wants to marry one of the "satisfiers," or women given over completely to lovemaking, and she tells him to beat it.

Many have rated this film very highly, largely because of the superior treatment of the erotic scenes, but the science fiction story line is a tired subject and so predictable that it almost seems unnecessary.

Genre: Graphic
Year: 1981
Time: 82 min.
Acting: Good
Casting: Very Good

Script: Fair
Production: Good
Directing: Fair
Theme: Futuristic
Humor: No

★ Watchable ★★★ Must See
★★ Recommended ★★★★ Masterpiece

S

SATYRICON ★★★★

Director: Federico Fellini
Cast: Martin Potter, Hiram Keller, Max Born, Fanfulla

This is probably Fellini's most visually engaging film, and is without a doubt one of the masterpieces of film art. He weaves us through a tapestry of decadence during the Roman Empire with such stunning juxtapositions of brilliant images from a collapsing society that one cannot help but be reminded of our own times and its chaotic morality.

The film is freely adapted from Petronius' *Satyricon*, which is the exploits of two young Romans, Ascyltus and Encolpius, as they venture throughout the empire, indulging in both heterosexual and homosexual relationships. In the midst of this proliferation of sensuality, Ascyltus becomes impotent and madly searches for a remedy which ends in tragedy for Enclopius.

The film's treatment of the sexual decadence is remarkably powerful without being explicit. In fact, in light of the mental images it produces, it actually shows very little on screen. But there is a plethora of mysterious whores, hedonists, gluttons, and lechers. In the midst of this chaos, however, there is a beautifully light reprieve as the young Romans come across an abandoned villa. A very pretty slave girl has remained behind, and she playfully teases the two boys into an erotic encounter.

Otherwise, the sex is portrayed as bizarre, seductive, uncontrollable, mysterious, wicked, and excessive.

Genre: Erotic
Year: 1969
Time: 138 min.
Acting: Excellent
Casting: Excellent

Script: Very Good
Production: Excellent
Directing: Excellent
Theme: Decadence
Humor: No

SCENT OF HEATHER ★★★

Director: Philip Drexler Jr.
Cast: Veronica Hart, Paul Thomas, Vanessa Del Rio

High production standards, fine acting, and erotic situations make this a standout.

The story has overtones of the Italian movie *Till Marriage Us Do Part*, which is about two young people who marry, but before they can consummate the bond they discover that they might be brother and sister. Both are still very curious about the mysteries of sex and decide to mutually discover orgasm. Then they engage in sensual pastimes with the servants of their household.

The sex is quite realistic, mainly due to the superb acting talent of Veronica Hart. This film, incidently, was her first major part and proved that she could handle leading roles. Her portrayal of a girl's first sexual experience is an excellent example of good acting combined with intense eroticism.

The story is set in Victorian times and the photography captures the mood with skill and artistry.

Genre: Graphic
Year: 1981
Time: 99 min.
Acting: Very Good
Casting: Good

Script: Very Good
Production: Very Good
Directing: Very Good
Theme: Sexual Awakening
Humor: No

★ Watchable   ★★★ Must See
★★ Recommended   ★★★★ Masterpiece

S

SCREWPLES ★★

Director: Clair Dia
Cast: Kandi Barbour, Serena, Jamie Gillis

Screwples approaches the adult format from a slightly different angle, but the core is still the same.

A TV newswoman conducts random interviews on the street. The subject of her survey is erotic fantasies. People are only too willing to divulge their most hidden sex secrets to this beautiful young woman. The film then cuts to live-action as the interviewed person plays out his erotic dream.

After the lead-in, we are given the same old adult stuff. Director Dia has a flair for the erotic sequences, having been a sex performer herself. She knows what feels authentic on screen and what doesn't work, but her overall storytelling techniques are a little raw.

Kandi Barbour, the interviewer, is cute and daffy, but fits the male fantasy of what a luscious television live-action news reporter should look like.

Genre: Graphic
Year: 1979
Time: 72 min.
Acting: Good
Casting: Fair

Script: Fair
Production: Fair
Directing: Good
Theme: Newslady
Humor: Yes

SECRETS OF A WILLING WIFE ★★

Director: Norman Gerney
Cast: Merle Michaels, Rikki O'Neal, Eric Edwards

While not great, this film does have a certain charm to it, especially in the glib style of the performances.

A housewife finds her husband in the sack with her best friend and she decides to get even by bedding the first man she finds. In the process, she discovers she likes this adventurous lifestyle and begins to experiment more, finally ending in divorce and a new hobby for her.

The sex is typically long and varied as the woman pursues her lusty sideline, going from one man, group, or woman to another. The cast has so much fun while performing that the audience begins to identify with the characters in a strangely erotic way.

The film is reluctantly charming, as evidenced by the way the young housewife effortlessly tosses a line to her psychologist, "I'm having a party in my mouth."

Genre: Graphic
Year: 1980
Time: 78 min.
Acting: Good
Casting: Fair

Script: Fair
Production: Fair
Directing: Fair
Theme: Housewife
Humor: Yes, of Sorts

★ Watchable ★★★ Must See
★★ Recommended ★★★★ Masterpiece

S

THE SEDUCTION OF LYNN CARTER

Director: Wes Brown
Cast: Andrea True, Jamie Gillis, Sharon Thorpe

A raunchy film that portrays sex purely from the male point of view, often becoming abusive.

A happy, normal woman happens to meet a sex scholar while visiting her dentist. They strike up a conversation, and he offers her lunch the next day. For the fun of it—and being curious—she accepts, and thus begins her sexual odyssey.

At first, she rejects the man's advances, but soon she gives in. The beginning is simply an extramarital affair, but it quickly disintegrates into a passion for more and weirder sensual games culminating in her absolute humiliation.

The sex is quite varied, but carefully orchestrated. As an adult film, it is potent and might not appeal to many because of its ill treatment of women. It does, however, attempt to show a dark side of the female psyche that may or may not be part of some women's erotic fantasies.

Genre: Graphic	**Script:** Fair
Year: 1974	**Production:** Fair
Time: 84 min.	**Directing:** Good
Acting: Very Good	**Theme:** Sex Education
Casting: Good	**Humor:** No

SEKA

While it was not her first film, Seka's popularity soared when she appeared in Blonde Fire. Since then, this chesty platinum blonde has developed quite a strong and loyal following. With the advent of videocassettes, she is getting letters from both men and housewives asking for sexual advice. She is a video freak, and collects tape and equipment like kids collect comic books.

Seka currently lives in Chicago, but had previously lived in Hollywood where she actively pursued an erotic film career. She is a woman that knows where her talents lie, and has capitalized on them with the shrewdness of J. P. Morgan.

She has starred in Prisoner of Paradise; Plato's, The Movie; "F"; Downstairs/Upstairs; Blondes Have More Fun; Between the Sheets; Anytime, Anyplace; and did an on-screen interview for the recent adult documentary Exhausted, where, in contrast to all the other women interviewed, she said that John Holmes's most obvious asset was just right.

S

SENSATIONAL JANINE

Director: Hans Billian
Cast: Patricia Rhomberg, Linda Rogers, Irene Silver

This foreign film has become very popular in the States, largely due to the leading lady's wonderfully sensual performance and her abundant figure.

The story is based on a real turn-of-the-century woman, Josephine Mutzenbacher, who became a famous London madam. The movie chronicles her life, from her first experience with eroticism to her eventual obsession with selling her body, and finally to the setting up of her own brothel.

Sex is portrayed as a delightful intrigue. Much of the graphic shots seem to have been inserted, but Patricia Rhomberg's adorable curiosity about the sensual arts will warm the cockles of most men's hearts. Even prostitution has been romanticized to where the women are curiosity seekers and eager pleasure givers.

Sensational Janine has been considered by a number of adult film reviewers as one of the best foreign adult films released in the United States.

Genre: Graphic
Year: 1979
Time: 116 min.
Acting: Very Good
Casting: Good

Script: Good
Production: Very Good
Directing: Good
Theme: Prostitution
Humor: No

★ Watchable ★★★ Must See
★★ Recommended ★★★★ Masterpiece

SERENA   *aka Serena Blacquelourd*

As a teenager, Serena ran away from home. She ended up in Los Angeles with no money, no skills, but a very shrewd intellect. She got a job as a waitress, and was quickly discovered by a make-up artist. Her first adult film was The Journey of O and was quickly cast in Honeypie and Sweet Cakes.

Her red hair, sensual attractiveness, and fairly competent acting ability make her quite popular. Her most challenging role was the twin sisters in Ecstasy Girls, where she played both roles. One was a quiet, sensual woman, the other a loud, aggressive, kinky practitioner of off-beat sex. Other films Serena has starred in are Taxi Girls, N. Y. Babes, Blonde In Black Silk, The Sensuous Detective, Screwples, Heavenly Desire, Damiano's People, 800 Fantasy Lane, Afternoon Delights, Extremes, and Dracula Sucks. She has retired from the adult industry, but recently did a walk on for Damiano's Never So Deep and Carol Connor's Desire for Men.

S

SERENA—AN ADULT FAIRY TALE

Director: Fred Lincoln
Cast: Serena, China Leigh, Jamie Gillis

This is basically a profile of the adult film actress Serena, but it undoubtedly has been greatly altered. In fact, the film is really a modern-day adult version of Cinderella.

Serena plays a love object in a house of pleasure, where she is used over and over for other people's jollies. Somewhere in the midst of all this abuse, she is visited by her fairy god-mother, goes to the ball, snatches the handsome prince, and lives ever-after consumed with lust.

The story contains a lot of lesbianism, as Serena is toyed with and worked over by her lecherous sisters. There is also some mild bondage and humiliation, but that is to be expected from Serena who is constantly cast in offbeat erotic situations.

The film really doesn't come off as a film, but more as a vehicle for a lot of strong sex scenes. Serena is not a great actress, but she is a terrific sensual emoter.

Genre: Graphic
Year: 1979
Time: 72 min.
Acting: Fair
Casting: Fair

Script: Fair
Production: Poor
Directing: Fair
Theme: Fairy Tale
Humor: Yes

SEVEN INTO SNOWY

★½

Director: Antonio Shepherd
Cast: Abigail Clayton, Kay Parker, Paul Thomas

Not the most original idea but a fair improvement over previous Snow White takeoffs, with good performances by its leading ladies, Abigail Clayton and Kay Parker.

Parker plays Fedora, the evil stepmother, who tries to gain control of her stepchild, Snowy Weatherly, by first abusing her with magic spells. But when her mirror tells her that Snowy is the "sexiest of them all," Fedora gets mad and tries to humiliate Snowy sexually. Snowy's carnal lusts are so potent, however, that Fedora's efforts are like trying to put out a fire with gasoline.

While both Clayton and Parker are very sensual and sexually energetic performers, the film does tend to underplay them, and sometimes gets tedious. But the windup scene where Snowy takes on the Magnificent Seven motorcycle gang is terrific.

The film is sprinkled with erotic moments and mild good humor, but this one isn't likely to be on anyone's Top 20.

Genre: Graphic
Year: 1977
Time: 79 min.
Acting: Fair
Casting: Good

Script: Fair
Production: Fair
Directing: Fair
Theme: Fairy Tale
Humor: No

★ Watchable   ★★★ Must See
★★ Recommended   ★★★★ Masterpiece

S

SEX BOAT ★★

Director: Svetlana
Cast: Kelly Nichols, Kandi Barbour, Randy West

This is basically a re-telling of an already bad idea, TV's *The Love Boat*. It does, however, have some good erotic sequences and is somewhat entertaining.

Two stowaways hide out on an all-woman luxury liner. Naturally, many ladies are intrigued by the two and indulge themselves with great abandon. The guys are finally found out and tossed into the brig, but later released to help fight some pirates.

The premise allows a lot of sexual situations and the makers of this picture capitalize on it with great zeal. Randy West and Robert Lyon do a nice job playing two roosters in a henhouse. The movie is packed with gorgeous model-types in smart naval suits giving it a titillating quality, but the movie is more silly than funny.

Genre: Graphic
Year: 1980
Time: 80 min.
Acting: Fair
Casting: Fair

Script: Fair
Production: Good
Directing: Fair
Theme: Female Sailors
Humor: Yes

SEX ROULETTE ★★★

Director: Alan Vydra
Cast: Robert Leray, Vanessa, Desire Bastareau

This German film is a swift and erotic satire of the international gambling jet set.

Lord Robert de Chamoix was once a big-time gambler. He has won so much money in the casinos of Monte Carlo, San Remo, and Nizza that he's now retired, basking in the pleasures of beautiful, full-figured women. His live-in niece is coming of age, and wants desperately to express her budding sexuality. The uncle wants to help, and they enter a series of wildly wicked erotic games, taking them both into the gambling high life.

The women are orally fixated. A white maid tends to the needs of a black dwarf, a busty masseuse enjoys her work, and the maid takes care of her boss while he's watching television. There is plenty of lesbianism, incest, voyeurism, threesomes, groups, pregnant women in leather, and virgins being deflowered.

The high production values offer a lot of room for smooth editing. While much of the film centers on sex alone—with little thought to the story line—*Sex Roulette* is still a very interesting and entertaining adult fantasy.

Genre: Graphic
Year: 1977
Time: 115 min.
Acting: Fair
Casting: Very Good

Script: Fair
Production: Very Good
Directing: Good
Theme: Maids, Virgins
Humor: Yes

★ Watchable ★★★ Must See
★★ Recommended ★★★★ Masterpiece

S

SEX WORLD ★★½

Director: Anthony Spinelli
Cast: Lesllie Bovée, Kent Hall, Kay Parker, John Leslie

For its lush production and some involving sexual encounters, this movie rates high, but it fails to live up to its potential.

The story is a sexy takeoff of the popular film *Future World*, but also has a lot in common with the television series *Fantasy Island*. In this case, sexually disoriented people come to the resort for three days and nights. The film gives the audience bits and pieces of the characters, crosscutting between them as they have their erotic adventures. Tying the various episodes together is a mysterious control room where the guests are monitored.

Most of the sex is the standard adult formula, but the performances are better than most in spite of an occasional slip into melodrama. There is the typical lesbian scene, quasi-rape interlude, interracial lust, and others.

The film has some nice sets, high production values, and simulates—in many ways—what one would find on prime-time television. But the film doesn't live up to its science-fiction billing.

Genre: Graphic
Year: 1978
Time: 90 min.
Acting: Good
Casting: Good

Script: Fair
Production: Very Good
Directing: Good
Theme: Sex Therapy
Humor: No

SOMETIME SWEET SUSAN ★★

Director: Fred Donaldson
Cast: Harry Reems, Shawn Harris, Neil Flangager

The idea behind this film is solid, but the development is tedious with only an occasional bright spot.

A mental patient has explicit sex fantasies about her doctor. To complicate matters, the patient also has a second personality. Susan, the first personality, is sweet and soft-spoken, but Sandra, the second personality, is crusty, frank, and embittered. The story revolves around the efforts of a good-natured doctor to help the young girl come to grips with her highly sexed past.

The sex is quite romantic, but explicit all the same. It is always accompanied by sweet, swelling music to hide the fact that the erotic scenes drag on and on. Particularly effective is a two-girl encounter and a flashback of Susan making love to her old boyfriend. Sandra, on the other hand, has a penchant for raunch.

Shawn Harris has a stunning body, which was featured in *Gallery* magazine some time ago. As an actress she isn't bad, but this was her first and last film.

Sometime Sweet Susan was the first union-made adult film because of the number of Broadway actors who appeared in it.

Genre: Graphic
Year: 1974
Time: 86 min.
Acting: Good
Casting: Good

Script: Fair
Production: Good
Directing: Fair
Theme: Hospital Patient
Humor: No

★ Watchable   ★★★ Must See
★★ Recommended   ★★★★ Masterpiece

S

GEORGINA SPELVIN

Georgina Spelvin was at a mature age when she appeared in her first adult film, The Devil In Miss Jones. Like many actresses in the business, she did not set out to become an adult-film star. She was involved in the New York theater world and was a friend of Harry Reems. Through him, she got work behind the camera in some of the adult films.

Reems suggested to Gerard Damiano, a director, to consider Georgina in a film. Damiano was impressed with her acting, but didn't quite know about the rest of her. He cast her anyway, and the film—The Devil In Miss Jones—suddenly took off. With its success, Georgina established herself as a competent actress who is also very capable of handling explicit sex. She has won six Eroticas, two for Best Actress and four for Best Supporting Actress.

Her most memorable films are Desires Within Young Girls; Wet Rainbow; The Ecstasy Girls; Ping Pong; Take-Off; The Dancers; For Richer, For Poorer; Mystique; and The Private Afternoons of Pamela Mann.

Contrary to popular belief, she continues to work in adult films, and is currently working in a sequel to The Devil In Miss Jones.

ANNIE SPRINKLE   *aka Anny Sands*

Annie Sprinkle is not only involved in the adult-film world as an actress, but has had some success as a reporter, photographer, and columnist as well. She has written for most of the major men's magazines. She also claims that she would never write for a straight magazine even if they paid her a million bucks.

As her name implies, Annie is into water sports. That and other interests have earned her the title: America's First Lady of Kink.

Before acting, she worked behind the scenes doing set decoration, being a camera assistant, and a script girl. Harry Reems was instrumental in getting Annie her first acting break.

She has appeared in many films, including The Affairs of Janice; For Richer, For Poorer; Honeypie; Jack 'n Jill; Pandora's Mirror; Satan Was a Lady; The Satisfiers of Alpha Blue; Centerfold Fever; and Seduction. She recently wrote and directed herself in Deep Inside Annie Sprinkle.

S

STAR VIRGIN ★★½

Director: Linus Gator
Cast: Kari Klark, Tracy Walton, Jeanette Harlow

A very funny and erotic science-fiction spoof. It is nicely done, with some very erotic performances by the women.

The plot is divided into four loosely connected short stories. The last earthwoman is cast into deep space in her starship. Having never been on earth, she is curious, especially about an odd cultural phenomenon called sex. A cute robot displays four vignette accounts of this subject, and the woman watches with utter fascination.

The first one is about a '50s Garden of Eden. The second is about a sexy Dracula. There's a hilarious spoof of America's obsession with football and sex, especially as the two are mixed. Last is a strip show that ends in a backstage orgy.

Each segment is essentially a tightly spun erotic story, containing some very superior erotic performances. Kari Klark does some very exotic things with the robot as the machine demonstrates to her what "stimulation" is all about.

The film is alluring, attractive, and quite entertaining.

Genre: Graphic
Year: 1979
Time: 78 min.
Acting: Good
Casting: Good

Script: Good
Production: Very Good
Directing: Good
Theme: Science Fiction
Humor: Yes

STORY OF JOANNA ★★★

Director: Gerard Damiano
Cast: Terri Hall, Jamie Gillis, Zebedy Colt

With the success of *The Story of O*, master erotic filmmaker Gerard Damiano attempted his own version of female domination.

Jamie Gillis plays a suave, charming man who hates women. After wining, dancing, and romancing a lady, he lures her into his room of "forbidden treasures," which, in effect, are elaborate torture devices and techniques. He humiliates, degrades, and sexually abuses any female naive enough to fall for his lines.

The sex is brutal, graphic, and filled with pain, but Damiano does it with such craft that one can't help but become involved with the performances. In fact, actress Terri Hall seems to be enjoying herself, which makes the bondage scenes oddly erotic.

One of the bright spots in this moody, murky S & M story is a superbly choreographed ballet performed by Terri Hall, who used to dance for the Stuttgart Ballet Company. It is one of the very few well-executed erotic dance sequences ever in an adult film.

Also, there is a short, poignant homosexual encounter, not surprising for a film about a woman-hater.

Genre: Taboo	**Script:** Good
Year: 1975	**Production:** Good
Time: 86 min.	**Directing:** Very Good
Acting: Good	**Theme:** Torture
Casting: Very Good	**Humor:** No

★	Watchable	★★★	Must See
★★	Recommended	★★★★	Masterpiece

S

THE STORY OF O ★★★

Director: Just Jaeckin
Cast: Corinne Clery, Udo Kier, Anthony Steel, Jean Gaven

Like *Emmanuelle* this French movie was critically controversial, but has been very popular in the States. It is lush, nicely photographed, and Corinne Clery is quite appealing as a sensual actress.

The film is an adaptation of Pauline Reage's novel about a young girl called O and her entry into the art of loving. The particular philosophy here is that women, by nature, are inferior to men and should therefore submit to their every whim and desire. This is the only way for a woman to find ecstasy. O falls in love with a practitioner of this doctrine, and is forced to go through quite a lot before he will take her in.

The treatment of eroticism is careful and deliberate. O is initiated into a house of bondage where the women are playthings for the male clientele. No talking or complaining is allowed. If the rules are broken, they are "punished" in the cellar with whips and chains.

One can call this film a lot of things, but "subtle" isn't one of them. Still, it's not overly offensive either, despite its extremely one-sided view of femininity. It does have a seductive quality, and we are drawn into its exotic premise largely because of Corinne Clery's beauty and sensuality.

Genre: Erotic
Year: 1975
Time: 112 min.
Acting: Very Good
Casting: Good

Script: Fair
Production: Very Good
Directing: Good
Theme: Submission
Humor: No

SUPERVIXENS   ★★★

Director: Russ Meyer
Cast: Shari Eubank, Charles Pitts, Charles Napier

After a brief stint working within the Hollywood filmmaking community, Russ Meyer returned to his independent, big-busted, low-budget, high-energy style of filmmaking with *Supervixens.*

After the brutal murder of his promiscuous wife, Clint is forced to flee a small town. Harry, a wicked look-alike who committed the killing, had little trouble pinning the murder on Clint.

On the lam, Clint falls into a number of adventures, getting caught in the act with the mail-order wife of a farmer, having a brief affair with a chesty black mute girl, and finally coming across a diner/gas station run by a lonely but beautiful woman who turns out to be a copy of his former wife. Clint stays on at the diner to help out the woman, and falls in love. The killer, however, passes through, discovers Clint, kidnaps his new girlfriend, and tries to kill them both.

The women in *Supervixens* are buxom, attractive, and very intelligent, whereas the men are generally sex-crazed, vicious, and uncoordinated. Mayer usually bombards his audience with erotic images—big breasts, eager women, and simulated lovemaking—but here he gets carried away with several sadistic scenes that are real turn-offs.

Genre: Erotic	**Script:** Good
Year: 1975	**Production:** Very Good
Time: 105 min.	**Directing:** Very Good
Acting: Good	**Theme:** Housewife, Farm Girl
Casting: Very Good	**Humor:** Yes

★	Watchable	★★★	Must See
★★	Recommended	★★★★	Masterpiece

S

SWEET CAKES ★★

Director: Hans Johnson
Cast: Jennifer Wells, Linda Wong, Eric Edwards

Nude photography has been a long-time favorite of adult filmmakers, and *Sweet Cakes* is a good but highly flawed example.

A young female reporter (Wells) interviews a successful photographer (Edwards), and the story becomes a series of erotic vignettes told in flashback.

There is a tremendous amount of sex in this film. Eric turns photo sessions into orgies, and when he is accosted by gorgeous girls he ends up playing more than working.

While the film is not an accurate portrayal of the life of a photographer, it does live up to the fantasy. The erotic performances are energetic and lively. Wells, who has done very few adult films, is exquisite.

Genre: Graphic
Year: 1976
Time: 85 min.
Acting: Fair
Casting: Fair

Script: Fair
Production: Good
Directing: Fair
Theme: Models
Humor: Yes

SWEET CAPTIVE ★★

Director: Leoni Vallentino
Cast: Rhonda Jo Petty, John Holmes, Paul Thomas

For the sort of film it is, *Sweet Captive* does a fairly nice job. Rhonda Jo Petty is sweet and very likable and some of the situations are quite erotic, but the film is uneven overall.

A young man owes a big debt to a couple of his friends, and in exchange for the money, he offers his girlfriend as a sexual slave to cater to their sexual whims and fetishes. The boy talks to the girlfriend, asking her if she wants to participate in a really weird party, and she willingly agrees to go along.

The captive scenes are rich and abundant in sexual education. An innocent viewer will discover all the various ways two intelligent men can sensually interact with a pretty, young lady. The film uses various sex aids and experiments in bondage. A lot of it is quite erotic and playful, but sometimes just goes on too long.

Genre: Graphic	**Script:** Fair
Year: 1979	**Production:** Fair
Time: 78 min.	**Directing:** Good
Acting: Fair	**Theme:** Submission
Casting: Good	**Humor:** Yes

★	Watchable	★★★	Must See
★★	Recommended	★★★★	Masterpiece

S

SWEET MOVIE

Director: Dusan Makavejev
Cast: Carole Laure, Pierre Clementi, Anna Prucnal

When this film was first released, it was greeted with much criticism. Despite its controversy, some critics hailed it as the most interesting and progressive film of the year. It has since become a cult classic, but has never really been widely distributed.

The twofold story concerns the adventures of a young Canadian virgin marrying an American multi-millionaire contrasted with a Russian sailor meeting a young female revolutionary who is working on a barge in Amsterdam.

The adventures are swiftly paced, energetic and hilarious. The film has been criticized mainly for its uninhibited portrayal of various bodily functions: urination, defecation, and regurgitation mixed in with a lot of zany sexual antics.

Makavejev, who also directed *WR—Mysteries of the Organism* and *Montenegro,* has a deft ability to portray social taboos in a humorous light while keeping his characters consistent.

Of his three major films, *Sweet Movie* is the most cluttered, but like the others it is so filled with life, so exuberant, and so vibrant that many of its ambiguities don't seem to matter.

Genre: Taboo
Year: 1974
Time: 100 min.
Acting: Very Good
Casting: Very Good

Script: Good
Production: Very Good
Directing: Excellent
Theme: Virgins
Humor: Yes

TABOO ★★★

Director: Kirdy Stevens
Cast: Kay Parker, Mike Ranger, Dorothy LeMay

This very interesting film has become extremely popular in the videocassette market. Its success is primarily due to the leading lady, Kay Parker. She gives a fine portrayal of a very erotic woman.

A wife whose husband has just left her (for his cute, blonde secretary) sets out to find love and affection, but her attempts end in disaster. One day, she happens into the bedroom of her teenage son and an arousing, sensual, incestual affair begins.

The sex is fairly standard, but better done—and more realistic—than in most adult films. There is a big group scene in particular that is quite wicked.

The son, played by Mike Ranger, is miscast. Ranger has trouble passing for a teenager, and his acting ability is often lacking. Kay Parker, on the other hand, is quite believable as the mother and from time to time gives quite a nice performance, especially during her sensual encounters.

Genre: Graphic
Year: 1980
Time: 90 min.
Acting: Good
Casting: Fair

Script: Good
Production: Good
Directing: Good
Theme: Incest
Humor: No

★ Watchable ★★★ Must See
★★ Recommended ★★★★ Masterpiece

T

TAKE OFF

Director: Armand Weston
Cast: Wade Nichols, Georgina Spelvin, Lesllie Bovée

For an adult film, this one is quite ambitious and actually pulls off many of its premises. The story is solid, the acting good, and the filmmaking quite creative.

The basic premise is *The Picture of Dorian Gray* by Oscar Wilde. In this case, the picture is a moving one and Darrin (Dorian) is a sex star from the twenties. He brings in a young lady whom he seduces. When she asks him about his youthful looks, he explains by showing her some film clips, ranging from the twenties to the present. In the clips, the character ages, and the real person stays young.

The film's charm comes in the way the clips are structured. They are explicit sex scenes, but are also spoofs of many classic movies.

Eric Edwards is not a great performer, but he is a solid one, and does a fine job spoofing some of the great actors, i.e., James Cagney and Marlon Brando. The director has a good eye for visuals and a talent for wringing solid, potent eroticism without becoming dull. *Take Off* is very entertaining, especially for admirers of movie history.

Genre: Graphic
Year: 1978
Time: 103 min.
Acting: Good
Casting: Good

Script: Very Good
Production: Very Good
Directing: Good
Theme: Movies
Humor: Yes

TALK DIRTY TO ME ★★★½

Director: Anthony Spinelli
Cast: John Leslie, Jesie St. James, Richard Pacheco

This film won an Erotica Award for being the year's best film, which it dearly deserved. The acting is very fine, the story well thought out, and the overall effect quite nice.

It is about a macho-looking young man who has an uncontrollable urge to use foul langugage in front of women. While most ladies are repulsed, many are turned on, and he ends up seducing them. His best friend and side kick, Lenny, is a dimwitted boy. When he tries to copy his mentor's technique, he gets into a lot of trouble.

The sex is quite involving because it grows out of the story, and not simply because it's an adult film. The action does not stop when the performers jump in bed. Instead, we are carried through the whole process of seduction by this fast, dirty-talking young man.

The production values are good, but not exceptional, which keeps the film from being a real knockout.

Genre: Graphic
Year: 1980
Time: 80 min.
Acting: Excellent
Casting: Very Good

Script: Very Good
Production: Good
Directing: Very Good
Theme: Foul Language
Humor: Yes

★ Watchable ★★★ Must See
★★ Recommended ★★★★ Masterpiece

T

TANGERINE ★★

Director: Robert McCallum
Cast: Cece Malone, Holly McCall, Lauri Blue, Angel Desmond

This is a generally entertaining film with a few built-in problems.

A mother uses her girls to blackmail some prominent men. The girls—Faith, Hope, and Charity—seduce particularly lustful men, then threaten to tell the world if they don't hand over some cash. Most men comply.

The story gets into a number of steamy situations, running through a number of varied sexual interludes. There is almost everything in the way of kinky sex, and the girls always seem to enjoy what they're doing.

The biggest problem with the picture is the girls themselves. They can't act and they're just too old to be playing teenagers. The mother, however, is a treat as an intelligent, lusty older woman.

The photography is good, but the direction is flat.

Genre: Graphic	**Script:** Fair
Year: 1979	**Production:** Good
Time: 90 min.	**Directing:** Fair
Acting: Fair	**Theme:** Young Girls
Casting: Poor	**Humor:** No

TAXI GIRLS   ★½

Director: Jaccov Jaacovi
Cast: Nancy Suiter, John Holmes, Candida Royalle

This film was crudely put together, but it contains some very nice looking girls, an occasionally funny joke, and a silly plot. The ineptitude in this film does not insult its audience, but rather makes it somewhat amusing.

It is about a group of hookers who get tossed into jail. While there, one of the girls gets an idea. Instead of walking the street looking for tricks, why not drive a taxi and cater to some exclusive vices at the same time.

We are led into a number of silly sex scenes as the girls seduce a loan officer, car dealer, and others. It also appeals to many of the traditional male fantasies, such as all hookers are really sweet down deep, and the many-girls-on-one-guy routine. The women do have fun and the men in the picture seem to respond favorably to their teasing. In fact, parts of this film really are erotic, but only to men.

The story could have used an overhaul. But it was intended as light comedy, and—despite its sledgehammer approach—it does have some nice moments.

Genre: Graphic   **Script:** Poor
Year: 1979   **Production:** Fair
Time: 87 min.   **Directing:** Poor
Acting: Fair   **Theme:** Prostitution
Casting: Fair   **Humor:** Yes

★	Watchable	★★★	Must See
★★	Recommended	★★★★	Masterpiece

T

TEENAGE FANTASIES

Director: Frank Spokeman
Cast: Rene Bond, Cindy Adams, Art Dolores

Rene Bond was one of the early sex stars in adult films, and she shines in this otherwise dismal movie that was quite popular in the early seventies.

To give the story some redeeming value, it tries to interject the advice and counsel of a psychologist regarding reproductive functions. Narrating is the luscious Rene Bond, who discusses the various ways human bodies can interlock. She does this while demonstrating some of her favorite forms of body contact.

Today, the film has lost its shock value and, aside from Bond's sensual tossing and licking of lips, the film is tedious.

It did create quite a stir in its time, and as a result of her performance in this film and others, Rene Bond gained many admirers.

Genre: Graphic	**Script:** Poor
Year: 1972	**Production:** Poor
Time: 70 min.	**Directing:** Poor
Acting: Fair	**Theme:** Sex Education
Casting: Fair	**Humor:** No

THERESE AND ISABELLE ★★★

Director: Radley Metzger
Cast: Essay Persson, Gael

This was a milestone for erotic films. It was a serious attempt to show the budding sexuality of two schoolgirls and did not try to exploit its premise. Even by today's standards, the film is interesting and provocative.

Therese and Isabelle are both attending the same girl's school. Therese is energetic, smart, and becomes a mentor for the innocent, naive, sweet Isabelle. She guides her through a number of exotic experiences, including a trip through an exclusive brothel, into her first lesbian liaison, and indirectly into her first heterosexual experience.

The film does not exploit any sex, nor is there an abundance of nudity. The imagery is effective, but sometimes the camera lingers too long, and the story lags.

The director, Radley Metzger, went on to make a number of explicit erotic films under the name of Henry Paris (*The Opening Of Misty Beethoven, Naked Came the Stranger*, etc.)

Metzger/Paris is perhaps one of the most significant of the erotic filmmakers. He always has extremely detailed stories, good acting, and very high standards of cinematography.

Artistically, however, this is perhaps his most solid. His later attempts catered toward entertainment, whereas *Therese and Isabelle* was a study into the nature of youthful eroticism.

Genre: Erotic
Year: 1968
Time: 118 min.
Acting: Very Good
Casting: Very Good

Script: Fair
Production: Good (b/w)
Directing: Good
Theme: School Girls
Humor: No

★ Watchable ★★★ Must See
★★ Recommended ★★★★ Masterpiece

T

3 AM ★★★

Director: Robert McCallum
Cast: Georgina Spelvin, Rhonda Gallard, Clair Dia

A very well made adult film with fine dramatic performances, top-notch all around.

It is about a woman who goes to live with her sister's family. She narrates the film, and in flashback we see how she caused the family to eventually split apart.

The film is realistic and so is the sex. The sensual attraction between performers is electric, but it does not dominate the film. Character development is smooth and careful. There is incest, lesbianism, a mysterious stranger, and a lot of sex on a boat.

Clair Dia does a fine job for a performer not noted for her acting ability. Much of the lighting is moody and in keeping with the seductive nature of the film.

Genre: Graphic
Year: 1976
Time: 90 min.
Acting: Very Good
Casting: Good

Script: Good
Production: Good
Directing: Very Good
Theme: Seduction
Humor: No

THROUGH THE LOOKING-GLASS ★★★½

Director: Jonas Middleton
Cast: Catharine Burgess, Jamie Gillis, Terri Hall

This is a pip. It doesn't get top rating because it's a little slow in the beginning and switches its premise halfway through, a disorienting move.

The title may be a little misleading. It is more about Dante's *Inferno* than it is a sequel to *Alice In Wonderland*, but it does have some of those delightful aspects. It is about a rich and beautiful woman who's in love with herself.

Obsessed with her own image, she sits in front of a full-length mirror for hours primping herself, gazing at her nude body, and masturbating. She spends so much time there that she begins to have bizarre fantasies, some in which a demon comes out of the mirror and rapes her. She is so taken by these fantasies that she passes through the mirror and into a world crazed with sensuality.

While it is an adult film, the sex is not as indulgent as in most adult movies. The story spends a lot of time on the woman and in developing her declining psychology.

The ending sequence takes place in a nightmare (distinguished by some very effective cinematography and lighting). The characters in this ethereal world are certainly bizarre as they engage in one perversion after another. The appearance of the self-possessed beauty is just a slight distraction to them.

Burgess does a remarkable job in her role, showing that it was the character, not the actress, with the airy brain in the first three-quarters of the picture.

Genre: Graphic
Year: 1976
Time: 91 min.
Acting: Very Good
Casting: Very Good

Script: Good
Production: Good
Directing: Very Good
Theme: Bored Housewife
Humor: No

T

THE TIFFANY MINX ★★★

Director: Robert Walters
Cast: Samantha Fox, Marlene Willoughby, Merle Michaels,
Crystal Synk

Though the net effect of this film is really compelling, its craft
never quite matches the creativity of its raw ideas.

The story is about a young woman, Jessica Grover, who has
just inherited a fortune upon the death of her father. But Jessica's husband, wanting the estate for himself, hires a hit man
to get rid of her. The plot is further complicated when the hit
man decides to rape her first and in the process she knocks
him off with a pair of scissors.

The harsh juxtaposition of soft erotic scenes and brutal
rape/violence is jarring. The onslaught of images is quite effective and makes for a very bumpy ride, which unintention-
ally improves the film.

The performances are very good, especially Crystal Synk
and Samantha Fox. Fox has a way of combining stupidity and
evil that is unnerving.

As a mystery, the film still works, but many of its fine points
have been muddied by unclear plotting and an odd blend of
gore and eroticism.

Genre: Graphic   **Script:** Good
Year: 1981   **Production:** Good
Time: 85 min.   **Directing:** Fair
Acting: Good   **Theme:** Murder Mystery
Casting: Good   **Humor:** No

★ Watchable   ★★★ Must See
★★ Recommended   ★★★★ Masterpiece

TRASH ★★

Producer: Andy Warhol
Director: Paul Morrissey
Cast: Joe Dellesandro, Holly Woodlawn, Jane Forth

Trash is Andy Warhol's outrageously deadpan look at New York lowlife. It is an appealing film with some oddly adorable characters. But it has very little filmmaking quality.

Joe and Holly are slum dwellers. She collects junk furniture while he burglarizes upper-class apartments. He's a drug addict and she's a nymphomaniac. He's impotent and she's frustrated. We are taken through a number of very funny scenes in an almost documentary approach. We see Joe being taunted by a sweet whore, but he can't get aroused. Holly's big dream is to get on welfare, and she fakes being pregnant to fool a welfare investigator (who opens the conversation by saying, "You look like a couple of respectable hippies").

The nudity and sex in the film, which is frequent, is not intended to arouse or stimulate the audience. The performers are more pathetic than attractive. The sex is used, rather, to unbalance the viewers and to move us much more intimately and realistically into these people's lives.

Even though it came from the avant-garde filmmaking community, *Trash* played to a broad audience. It was significant in its time in that it widened what previous films had dealt with in regards to sex and drug addiction. And it does so without preaching. *Trash* was the first film to present realistically disgusting characters without apologizing for them.

Genre: Taboo
Year: 1970
Time: 103 min.
Acting: Very Good
Casting: Very Good

Script: Fair
Production: Poor
Directing: Good
Theme: Impotence
Humor: Yes

T

TROPIC OF DESIRE ★

Director: Bob Chinn
Cast: Georgina Spelvin, Jesie St. James, Kitty Shane

While this film is no blockbuster of erotic entertainment, it is a credible adult film.

It takes place in the Pink Flamingo whorehouse of Honolulu. The time is the last days of World War II. The number one girl of the joint, Rita, learns that her lover has just been killed, and decides to move back to the States. Just as she leaves, a group of sex-starved sailors arrive.

The movie's premise lends much screen time to sexual activity. It lingers too long on the sex, and not enough time building and developing realism. It's a shame because the picture has some nice photography, an interesting environment, and some likable actors.

Genre: Graphic	**Script:** Poor
Year: 1979	**Production:** Good
Time: 90 min.	**Directing:** Fair
Acting: Fair	**Theme:** Brothel
Casting: Fair	**Humor:** No

TURKISH DELIGHT ★★★

Director: Paul Verhoeven
Cast: Monique van de Ven, Rutger Hauer, Tony Hurdeman

This is a delightful film that started out as an adult movie. The story is so good and the acting so superior that the second half becomes much more than just an exploitation film.

It begins with Eric, a sculptor and chronic woman-chaser, whose wife is dying of a brain tumor. Eric is so successful with the ladies that he begins collecting their hair, gluing it into his scrapbook. He comes across a striking redhead named Olga, whom he animalistically seduces in the car. Instead of clipping her hair, he falls in love with her and chases her all over Holland.

The treatment of sex is titillating and humorous. It is not graphic, but the performers are quite energetic and the erotic encounters are remarkably realistic.

It moves quickly from reality to sexual fantasies mixed with daydreams of killing, blood, and vengence. Despite these gross displays, the movie is so full of life and potent acting that it is more alluring than repelling.

Genre: Erotic
Year: 1973
Time: 102 min.
Acting: Excellent
Casting: Very Good

Script: Very Good
Production: Good
Directing: Excellent
Theme: Artist Models
Humor: Yes

★ Watchable ★★★ Must See
★★ Recommended ★★★★ Masterpiece

U

UNTAMED ★★

Director: Ramsey Karson
Cast: Kay Parker, Paul Thomas, Abigail Clayton

This is not really a bad adult film, but its average production values and loose plot keep it mediocre.

It is a loosely put together vignette film. The framing plot is a writer, gorgeously portrayed by Kay Parker, interviewing a hard-nosed private eye, played by Paul Thomas. He relates to her some of his most spectacular (and lusty) adventures.

The premise is just an excuse to give the viewer a lot of hot, steamy sex scenes, catering to just about every adult coupling legally available on film: lesbianism, group sex, and a variety of different positions. It's all standard stuff, really.

Abigail Clayton, Kay Parker, and Nancy Hoffman are enjoyable as sex performers, but unfortunately the film's story doesn't give them much in the way of character development. Paul Thomas does a solid job as the private detective, but this is not one of his more flashy roles.

Genre: Graphic
Year: 1977
Time: 80 min.
Acting: Good
Casting: Fair

Script: Fair
Production: Fair
Directing: Fair
Theme: Detective
Humor: No

★ Watchable ★★★ Must See
★★ Recommended ★★★★ Masterpiece

UP! ★★★

Director: Russ Meyer
Cast: Margo Winchester (Raven de la Croix), Kitten Natividad, Mary Gavin

While *Up!* is not one of Russ Meyer's more historically significant films, it is one where his special talents produce a near-perfect example of titillating erotica.

The film begins quite mysteriously in a dungeon where a young man is torturing an Adolf Hitler look-alike. We then quickly cut to a stunning nude, played by Kitten Natividad, who teasingly introduces the audience to the setting. We are in Northern California, in a small, rural community. Just outside of town, a very beautiful, buxom young lady is hitchhiking along a lonely country road. She is picked up by a young man, who happens to be the *enfant terrible* of the local rich set. He tries to take advantage of the girl's abundant sexuality, but after a short sequence involving a brutal rape, she turns the tables and ends up killing him.

Russ Meyer has never been one to linger too long on a single shot. He likes to cut, especially to ladies running naked as jaybirds around the lush countryside. In this case, however, he has added more than just a tease with Kitten Natividad, who narrates the events of the story with a husky, British accent while displaying her terrific figure. The true star of the show, however, is Margo Winchester (Raven de la Croix), whose piercing dark eyes and fully rounded, voluptuous figure combine with some staunch acting for an explosive performance.

Genre: Erotic
Year: 1976
Time: 84 min.
Acting: Very Good
Casting: Excellent

Script: Very Good
Production: Good
Directing: Very Good
Theme: Country Girls, Waitresses
Humor: Yes

U

URBAN COWGIRLS   ★½

Director: Tsanuski
Cast: Veronica Hart, Eric Edwards, Lee Carroll

Urban Cowgirls tied with *Talk Dirty To Me* for the Erotica Award's best picture. It is as average an adult film as *Talk Dirty* was superior. The Best Picture Award was a joke.

This is an adult version of *Urban Cowboy,* and is as dismally inspired as the original. Basically, it follows the lusty adventures of four phony cowgirls and their nightly carousing in a western dance hall called Billy's.

As a film, it never really takes off, but wallows in half-baked characterizations. The photography is nice, and it does a fine job in creating the mood and atmosphere of a smoke-filled bar.

Genre: Graphic	**Script:** Poor
Year: 1980	**Production:** Good
Time: 84 min.	**Directing:** Fair
Acting: Fair	**Theme:** Cowgirls
Casting: Good	**Humor:** No

V — THE HOT ONE ★★

Director: Robert McCallum
Cast: Annette Haven, John Leslie, Laurien Dominique

This movie is well-made but subpar in both its acting and its sex scenes.

It is about a woman who was molested as a young girl. Not understanding the girl's trauma, her mother labels her a whore. When she grows up, she marries a well-to-do man, but the psychological damage had been done. She suffers from a need to engage in sleazy, lowlife sex. By day she is a wealthy housewife, by night a cathouse hooker.

The sex scenes sometimes get downright raunchy, but the exquisite Annette Haven always tones them with a strange mixture of beauty and dirt. The eroticism contains a rich variation of sex, most of which is justified by the woman's crazed psychological desires.

The failing is in the performances. Annette Haven is a very beautiful girl and has done some nice acting, but she's not a super talent. Nor is the sex packed with intense, energetic lust —she's too dainty and fastidious.

Genre: Graphic
Year: 1978
Time: 95 min.
Acting: Fair
Casting: Good

Script: Good
Production: Good
Directing: Good
Theme: Prostitution
Humor: No

★ Watchable ★★★ Must See
★★ Recommended ★★★★ Masterpiece

V

VIXEN ★★

Director: Russ Meyer
Cast: Erica Gavin, Harrison Page, Garth Pillsbury

Vixen is a charming film filled with lovable people. It cemented Russ Meyer's reputation in cult-film circles.

Vixen Palmer is the wife of a Canadian bush pilot. She and her husband run a resort for vacationers, but she utilizes the place more for her erotic exploits than for making money. To say that she is promiscuous is an understatement. She taunts many of the young boys in a nearby town, and basically has a good time.

Everyone seems to know about Vixen's sexploits except her husband, who constantly considers her a loving, loyal housewife. The plot moves into high gear when a Communist hijacks the husband's plane and orders him at gunpoint to fly to Cuba.

While Meyer never moved into graphic sex, Vixen was one of the early formulative films for the adult market. It contained much simulated intercourse, a lot of nudity, and sex jokes. The film by nature is exploitative, but Meyer always lets the plot move in and out of the erotic encounters, creating a sublime titillating sex comedy rather than a series of cheap shots. The performances are always exuberant, and—despite the hilarious action—the characters are very realistic.

Genre: Erotic	**Script:** Good
Year: 1968	**Production:** Fair
Time: 71 min.	**Directing:** Very Good
Acting: Good	**Theme:** Housewife
Casting: Very Good	**Humor:** Yes

WEEKEND FANTASY ★

Directors: Vinnie Rosi and William Margold
Cast: Jennifer West, William Margold, Kathy Konners

Despite its brutal premise and ultra-low technique, this film has a strange allure to it. Very much a guilty pleasure.

It is about a sex club. A group of friends meet every weekend at a cabin to indulge in sensual perversion. The men use the women as sex objects. One day, the most dominant figure (William Margold) decides to do something really kinky. They pick a girl at random, kidnap her, and drag her to the cabin where she is repeatedly raped by both the men and the women.

The sex is brutal, sometimes sickening, but surprisingly free of gore and real physical damage. In fact, what they do to the girl is more psychological than physical. There are lots of ropes, whips, and chains.

The characters do not try to justify what they are doing, unlike the lush production of The Story of O, which is also about a young girl's excursion into bondage. In Weekend Fantasy, the characters know that what they're doing is wrong, but they have been so jaded by their perversions that they don't care.

Genre: Taboo
Year: 1980
Time: 80 min.
Acting: Poor
Casting: Fair

Script: Poor
Production: Poor
Directing: Very Poor
Theme: Rape
Humor: No

★ Watchable   ★★★ Must See
★★ Recommended   ★★★★ Masterpiece

RANDY WEST

Randy West has had a rich and varied past. He has been a waiter, salesman, flower delivery person, butcher, taxi driver, and supermarket stockboy. An early acting career included summer stock, commercials, and stage plays. But it was his job as an art school model that led to his auditioning for adult films. His first films were Her Name Was Lisa, Sex Boat, Bon Appetit, and American Pie, where he established himself as a fairly competent actor with an all-American, pretty-boy image.

He has since appeared in Bad Circle, Dracula Exotica, Sunny, The Dancers, The Filthy Rich, Between the Sheets, Country Comfort, Skintight, and the soon-to-be-released Titillation.

Randy is quickly establishing himself as one of the major actors of adult film, and seems to be doing a very good job at it.

WICKED SENSATIONS ★★½

Director: Ron Chrones
Cast: John Leslie, Annette Haven, Paul Thomas

This film has received a lot of recent acclaim and has been quite popular despite its rather trite story and mediocre acting.

John Leslie plays a writer whose book has just been bought by an adult filmmaker. His own sexuality, however, is a little peculiar—he likes to watch. He makes a deal with his next-door neighbor to look through his window while he (the neighbor) romps with a beauty in bed. The writer's wife, however, is a little put off by his sexual antics. The ill feelings force him out of the house and in pursuit of a woman he once glimpsed at the film producer's office.

The sex grows out of the plot, but is still overweighted and lingers endlessly. The setups, however, are carefully thought out as is the friendship between the writer and the playboy neighbor. In fact, John Leslie received the 1982 Erotic Award for Best Actor.

The cinematography is very professional and matches the quality of most television shows, but the bland story idea keeps this film from being great.

Genre: Graphic
Year: 1981
Time: 80 min.
Acting: Fair

Casting: Fair

Script: Fair
Production: Very Good
Directing: Good
Theme: Voyeurism, Female Hitchhikers
Humor: Yes

★ Watchable ★★★ Must See
★★ Recommended ★★★★ Masterpiece

W

W. R.—MYSTERIES OF THE ORGANISM ★★★½

Director: Dusan Makavejev
Cast: Milena Dravic, Jagoda Kaloper, Ivica Vidovic

Social taboos, erotica, and politics are blended in this hilarious work by a master of comic timing and sensual display.

The plot spins off of Wilhelm Reich's controversial Orgone Theories. (Reich was jailed for his unorthodox therapeutic techniques in the United States during the '50s.) Reich believes that unless a mysterious universal phenomenon called "orgone energy" is discharged naturally through sexual union, neurosis will erupt.

The film is a collection of these sorts of neuroses, done with exceptional craft and comic action, set in modern-day Yugoslavia. The main character is Milena Dravie, who shouts from her slum apartment: "Politics is for those whose orgasm is incomplete!" Complimenting the idealistic Milena are two female sexologists who are obsessed with the physical nature of human relations.

The film is a blast at repression of any kind—political or moral—and an ode to uninhibited sexual intercourse. Repression sickens and enslaves, whereas nature's physical pleasure sets the human spirit free.

The movie marks the first male erection in a major movie (albeit a foreign one) as one of the women makes a plaster cast of her favorite part of the male physique. There is an abundance of vivacious sexual encounters, much nudity, and constant dipping into other social taboos, but the film's coup de grace is a natural blending of erotica, humor, and politics.

Genre: Erotic	**Script:** Excellent
Year: 1971	**Production:** Very Good
Time: 70 min.	**Directing:** Very Good
Acting: Excellent	**Theme:** Sex Education
Casting: Very Good	**Humor:** Yes